Home, Family and Community

Kathleen Heasman
*Formerly Senior Lecturer in Social Studies,
Queen Elizabeth College, London University*

London
GEORGE ALLEN & UNWIN
Boston   Sydney

First published in 1978

This book is copyright under the Berne Convention. All rights are reserved. Apart from any fair dealing for the purpose of private study, research, criticism or review, as permitted under the Copyright Act, 1956, no part of this publication may be reproduced, stored in a retrieval system, or transmitted, in any form or by any means, electronic, electrical, chemical, mechanical, optical, photocopying, recording or otherwise, without the prior permission of the copyright owner. Enquiries should be addressed to the publishers.

© Kathleen Heasman, 1978

ISBN 0 04 301087 3

British Library Cataloguing in Publication Data

Heasman, Kathleen
   Home, family and community.
   1. Family – Great Britain
   I. Title
   301.42'1'0941   HQ613   77-30537

ISBN 0-04-301087-3

Photoset in 10 on 11 point Monophoto Times by
Northampton Phototypesetters Ltd
and printed in Great Britain by
Unwin Brothers Limited
The Gresham Press Old Woking Surrey

Contents

	page
Acknowledgements	4
Preface	5

1 *Home, Family and Social Class* — 7
  The Home
  The Family
  Society, Culture and Social Class
  The Contemporary British Family
  Immigrant Families

2 *The Family Group* — 23
  Personal Relationships
  The Establishment of a Family
  Children, their Development and Care
  Relationships within the Family
  The Single-Parent Family

3 *Earning and Spending* — 40
  The National Economy
  Earning an Income
  Consumer Spending
  Retail Marketing
  Consumer Interests

4 *Work and Leisure* — 62
  Work in Relation to Leisure
  Working Wives
  Leisure Activities
  Leisure Industries
  Planning for Leisure

5 *Housing the Family* — 79
  The Development of a Housing Policy
  The Present Housing Situation
  Housing Standards
  Types of Houses
  Housing for Specialised Groups

6 *The Family in a Community Setting* — 99
  Rural and Urban Areas
  Environmental Planning
  Problems of Urban Growth
  The Community and its Development
  Neighbourhood and Neighbours

4   *Home, Family and Community*

7 *Social Services for the Family*	*page* 122

    The Welfare State
    Special Provision for the Family
    Voluntary Organisations and Volunteers
    Socially Deprived Families
    The Development of a Sense of Responsibility

8 *Homes of the Future*	141
Further Reading	147
Index	149

Illustrations

The national economy (Figure 1)	41
Government expenditure for 1975 (Figure 2)	42
Household expenditure for 1976 (Figure 3)	47
Brent Cross shopping centre	55
Consumer protection marks	60
Slum housing	81
Lillington Gardens council estate	86
City structure: concentric zones (Figure 4)	100
City structure: sector pattern (Figure 5)	102
City structure: multiple nuclei pattern (Figure 6)	103
Aerial view of Birmingham	104
Street pollution	109
Neighbourhood centre at Hemel Hempstead	119

Acknowledgements

The author and publishers are grateful to the following for permission to reproduce illustrative material:
Brent Cross Shopping Centre (page 55); British Standards Institution, British Electrotechnical Approvals Board for Household Equipment (page 60); Shelter, National Campaign for the Homeless (page 81); Brecht-Einzig Ltd (pp. 100, 102-3); Birmingham Post Studios (page 104); Richmond and Twickenham Times (page 109); Commission for the New Towns (Hemel Hempstead) (page 119).

Preface

The definition of a home has always been somewhat ambiguous. It is usually regarded as a place where people live. Sometimes it is thought of as the place where the young are brought up. Occasionally it is regarded as the home circle or a household of people who live together.

The home is the centre of family life. It is there that relationships between family members are formed and developed. A home where relationships are good has a better chance of producing a happy and united family. They, in their turn, will hand on this capacity to form good relationships to their children, and so it will go on. But the material aspects of the home can impinge on the human aspects. If the home is substandard so that the mother is overworked, or if the children are constantly unwell because of poor living conditions, then however good the relationships within it, the home is unlikely to be very satisfactory.

Even if the material aspects of the home are adequate, the family still has to learn how to get on together, for it is composed of members who differ in age, personality and ability. In societies which we now label as primitive, the young learnt this by observing and taking part in all the community's activities. But children like ours, who are not raised within a large family network, may have little chance to get to know other age groups or to understand the situations they will meet in adult life. This may have to be done outside the family, by the school, the church, or any other social group they may join. Hence the importance of the environment in which the family lives and the contacts which are made with other people.

Even the traditional methods of home-making are no longer followed, largely because they are not known to modern young people. This is partly because many more women now go out to work after marriage and so have little opportunity to pass on what they learnt from their parents. Young people are left to make up their own minds as to how they will live their lives and this can be disconcerting both to them and to older generations. It is not surprising that in a recent survey by the National Children's Bureau, *Britain's Sixteen-Year-Olds*, more than half those questioned said they would like to know more about home-making and the problems of family life.

Our failure to prepare young people in these respects is seen in the increasing number of family breakdowns. This means that every year there are more children in our ostensibly compassionate society who grow up with little experience of family life.

Family life is studied in some schools as part of religious education, home economics or social studies. There are also projects like the

Schools Council Humanities Curriculum Project, and some very enterprising television series. But because far too many schools still regard such preparation for life as an optional extra, there is a great need for resource material which could be used and amplified by those seeking to fill this gap in our educational system.

The purpose of this book is to provide resource material of this kind. It sets out to show how inextricably interrelated are the affairs of the home, the family and the community. For the home is not just the place where domestic skills are practised, it is where family relationships are made and attitudes and beliefs formed. But a family which fails to look outside itself cannot perform these tasks adequately. It needs contact with the community as a whole, both for the resources which the community offers, and in order to make its own contribution to the life of the community.

This book is therefore concerned with the human and social aspects of the home. It covers the syllabuses of A level home economics under which these aspects of the home are studied, and also takes in some of the subject matter dealt with in general studies courses. It should also be of value to those concerned with people and their needs, including those training for nursing, the Christian ministry and similar professions.

It does not claim to be exhaustive, but only to touch on the various aspects of basic living. Other books are suggested to supplement the material given here if more detailed information is needed or the need is to study a subject in more depth. It itself, this book should enable the reader to gain a balanced background against which the life of the home and family can be better understood.

1 Home, Family and Social Class

Driving in the dusk through the countryside is always an exciting experience. Except for the car headlights, everything is in darkness. Then scattered patches of light appear, first from one or two outlying cottages, then from houses set fairly regularly on each side of the road. Some are large and stand in their own gardens. Others are smaller, linked together, each with its own patch of green in front. The lights are on now, but the curtains not yet drawn, so it is possible to see inside. People are gathered around the fireplace or sitting down to a meal, both children and adults, with perhaps a baby in a cot, a cat or dog curled up on the hearthrug, or a bird swinging in its cage. They are all there together, relaxed and enjoying one another's company. The house has been transformed into a home.

The Home
Originally the home was just a cave or a shelter in which people related to one another could live in safety and security. Here they were protected from others who might take their belongings or interfere with what they were doing. They were also protected from the weather, wild animals and other kinds of danger. People needed protection of this sort not only to preserve themselves, but so that they could eat and sleep in safety. So the home very soon became the place where food was brought when it had been gathered or caught, where it was prepared and where very simple cooking was done.

These early or primitive homes were usually some kind of hut construction, probably made by planting sticks in the ground in a circle, binding their tops together to form a cone, and covering the framework with thatch or leaves. The wigwam type, common to many American Indian tribes, is typical of this sort of home, although their covering was of skins rather than brush or leaves. Cooking was done in a pot in the middle of the wigwam, and there was possibly a hole at the top to let out the smoke.

Sleeping involved simply wrapping up in some animal's skin and lying on the floor, but in the daytime the skins were put to one side and the area was used for living. Such homes consisted of only one room, and if the occupants needed more space they just built more huts within a single enclosure, as in many Central African villages today.

At some ancient time the primitive cave dweller discovered that his cave could be enlarged by building a wall of piled rocks in front of it, and roofing the space between the cave and the wall with logs or skins. In this way it gradually became possible for some inhabitants to be allocated different parts of the dwelling to sleep in. Rooms began to be divided off and to be used for more specialised purposes and crude pieces of furniture were made on which to sit or lie or to gather round for meals. The idea of the home as a place of comfort began to evolve and as man's energies were no longer entirely devoted to keeping himself alive, he could make additional improvements in his home to make life more attractive. Such improvements were in the construction of the home, the way it was heated and furnished, the way food was prepared, cooked and served, and domestic activities such as washing and cleaning carried out.

These improvements were rather slow in developing because security against enemies and the hazards of the climate were still the most important things to be borne in mind when making a home. In the Middle Ages the homes of ordinary people still consisted of one-room hovels, clustered together for safety, below the feudal lord's castle walls. As feudalism decayed, the homes of the people began to improve, so that they came to consist of a few simple, screened areas with a fireplace in the centre, pitched roofs of thatch or slate and walls of various materials such as stone, timber and half timber. Examples of these can be seen in the folk museums which more and more countries are setting up.

A big change in the homes of working people came with the development of technology in the late nineteenth century. At first technological developments were used for the benefit of industry, but when people had to gather in large numbers in the towns to supply the labour for the new industries, it became possible to apply some of the developments to the home. Improvements were made in areas like drainage, sanitation and water supply which needed to be carried out on a large scale to make them sufficiently economical. Flush lavatories could now be built to replace the outdoor 'thunder-box' in common use in the more rural areas, and the chamber pots whose contents were collected daily by the night-soil cart in the densely populated towns. Gas lighting began to be used instead of the candle or oil lamp, and by the early decades of this century electricity had replaced gas in most homes. Cooking and heating which had previously used solid fuel such as wood, charcoal and coal, could now be done by gas and electricity. Many homes which were built after the First World War contained gas or electric cookers, while those built after the Second World War might possibly have central heating fired by gas, electricity, oil or solid fuel as their source of warmth.

The domestic use of electricity brought a vital change to the drudgery of keeping the home clean and tidy. It meant the use of a vacuum cleaner instead of brushes and brooms, the electric iron rather than the old-fashioned flat iron which had to be heated on the fire, and various other types of household equipment which helped the housewife in her daily tasks.

All these things helped to make the home a place of comfort and to introduce a very different way of living from that of the primitive cave or tent dweller. But this does not necessarily mean that the modern dwelling has become more of a home. A home means people as well as the structure or house in which they live. Security and comfort can make a house more of a home, but it will only do so if it helps the people in it to live a fuller and happier life together.

A home depends on the relationships between the people who live in it, usually people related to one another in some way. Most homes consist of the members of a family, father, mother and children, with perhaps a dependent relative, or even servants in some countries. They live in close contact with one another and so relationships have to be worked out. When these relationships are good, they produce a home atmosphere which enables all members of the household to relax, to be themselves and to do very much what they want. But if relationships are not good, then what could have been a home may remain just a place where people live.

A home means more than just those who live there together in comparative peace and happiness. There are also relatives and friends who do not live with the family and may only see them on rare occasions. For them the home is a focus to which they can return when in need or trouble, or when they want a rest or change. It is a place they can think about when they are far away and feel homesick, an image which gives them a sense of belonging when they are cut off from deep personal relationships with other people. To a serviceman, for instance, his most treasured possession is a photograph of his home and family.

So to some extent, a home is not dependent on the structure of the dwelling or its material comforts. The sense of a 'home' was as strong to the primitive dweller as it is to the family of today, living in a modern council house. But a comfortable dwelling does much to foster the feeling of a home. It helps the family to relax and to be themselves, it encourages relatives and friends to visit them and share their experiences. It is in the home that the family can make more wide-ranging relationships, discuss political, religious and other matters which concern the community at large, and learn to fit into the wider society of which it is a part.

A home, therefore, is a place, has a definite location, form, size and structure. But it also has an identity of its own which is determined by the people who live in it, their relationships with one another, with others in the neighbourhood and in society at large. It is impossible to study the physical structure, furnishings and planning of the home without considering the people who live in it. In fact the social and human aspects of home life are usually the factors which determine the ways in which the home is constructed, equipped and run.

The Family
The people who live in the home are usually members of a family. The family is important because everyone in society belongs to one. We are all born into a family and we usually marry, so forming a new branch of our family. It is our surname which indicates the family to which we belong, so that when they marry, women take the surname of, and join, the family of their husband. Even those who leave their family and have nothing to do with it are still family members and quite often return to their family in later life.

It is in the family that childhood experiences are gained. By the time other influences like the school or place of work begin to shape the individual in important ways, the family has already accomplished much of this basic transformation, having taught the child how to behave and play out many of the social roles which he or she will ultimately have to adopt. This process is known as 'socialisation' and it is the most important function of the family.

The human family possesses certain characteristics that facilitate this process of socialisation. The mother usually has only one child at a time, with a year or so between each child and the next. This means that there can be intense focus of attention on the behaviour of the infant when it is young, and this may gradually be withdrawn as other children come along. Sometimes the influence of the family lasts throughout life and so socialisation is spread over a long period. Nevertheless it is usually strongest when the child is young and at home. In later life a person may do what the family expects in certain things, but in others will follow his or her own way.

Some groups in society have tried to do without the family and to substitute instead their own special organisation. This has happened in the commune in China and the kibbutz in Israel. Here children are separated from their parents fairly soon after birth and brought up together. They rarely meet their parents and when they do, it is only for a short time. Those who have studied such children have found something lacking in them. The children were not responsive, they tended to be passive, listless and lacking in initiative. Only when the group contact was modified, and the children returned at night to sleep with their parents, did they become more like the children of an ordinary family.

This is rather like what happens in the communes of a modified type which are becoming popular in this country, especially among young and more adventurous families. Here all the children are together during the daytime, but they live with their parents and spend the weekends with them, and so have the advantages of the company of both their own age group and their parents.

A second purpose of the family is to produce children and so maintain the population. Parents are unlikely to be particularly concerned with the population problems of the society in which they live. They usually decide together in a very general way how many children they are going to have. But unwittingly, they will be influenced by the customs of their society. For instance, in a society where large families are greatly valued, or where children are needed to help with the work, the size of the family is likely to be big. But where the standard of living is regarded as important and family income is limited, parents begin to feel that a small family is preferable. Family size in such a society will gradually shrink and an increasing number of parents will conform to the customary pattern. Thus in Victorian times in this country, the typical family had four or five children. Now, two or three children are usual, although of course, some families have more or less than this number. The only child is often the result of a difficult first birth, while the very large family may be found where religion demands that parents should not limit the number of children they have.

A third function of the family is to maintain its members. Every family has to live and this means that its members must be fed, clothed and kept warm and comfortable. In some countries, like those of East Asia where families are engaged in farming, all the family members take part in this activity. Each member has his or her own special task, suited to age or ability. Together they produce most of the family needs and so are independent of others.

But in a modern urban society like our own, the situation is different. Most of what a family needs is produced by others and bought from the shops. It is the family income which is important. This is the prime responsibility of the father, and to a lesser extent of the mother and any other working members of the family. If the father is ill or not there, the family may find itself in difficulties. Hence the plight of many single-parent families.

A fourth function of the family is to provide the atmosphere of security and affection which is essential if the child is to grow up into a happy, adjusted human being. But it takes time for this to happen, because man, like other mammals, is helpless at birth and would die quickly without care. He is even worse off than most mammals in this respect because he matures later and so is unable to care for himself for quite a number of years. He has few instincts to help him adjust to his environment, and he has the most complex brain of all animals. Therefore he must be cared for in a group like a family that will feed, protect and help him to discover what he needs for the future. In such warm and sympathetic surroundings he should be able to develop normally and learn to be independent, so that he in his turn can teach his own family. If he has not this sense of security and affection he may never become emotionally mature, and this could mean that his children too will be deprived of a happy and affectionate home.

Not only does the relative importance of the functions of a family vary from one society to another, but the term 'family' itself can have somewhat different meanings. The basic characteristic of every family is that there is a blood relationship between its members, or what sociologists call 'kinship'. In some families this kinship relationship is recognised over a much wider area than in others. Where a very large number of distant relations are regarded as members of a family, the adjective 'extended' is used to describe the family; but where only fairly close relations are included in the family it is regarded as 'nuclear', this term implying that family members are fairly closely related to the nucleus of the parents.

The most usual form of the extended family is that which typically consists of several generations living together under one roof. This usually happens in the rural areas of countries like India, where many family members are needed to till the soil. An interesting example is found in the more remote parts of Sarawak, New Guinea, where several related families all live together in a single building called a 'longhouse'. Each nuclear family has its own room but there is a corridor down the middle where they all eat and meet together. In countries where the marriage custom of polygamy is followed and a man has several wives, it is quite usual for each wife and her children to have their own quarters in a tent or hut within the family compound.

The term 'extended family' can be used more loosely to describe a system of kinship relationships which are very close. Family members do not necessarily live together, though parents and near relatives usually do so. They are, however, in close and constant contact with one another and can easily be called upon in an emergency. Even if they are only distant cousins they feel a responsibility for the welfare of all the other family members. This is typical of many of the Africans and Asians who come to this country and who regard very distant relations as their 'cousins'.

One advantage of the extended family is its durability. Individuals come and go, but the family unit maintains its identity and its property, as well as its collective responsibility. The death or absence of a mother or father causes a rearrangement of duties rather than family breakdown. This is why students from overseas are not unduly distressed at leaving their young children behind, because they know that relatives will give them the care and affection they need. A further advantage is that people who live in extended families can usually turn to other family members in time of need. The old, the disabled and the sick are regarded as a family responsibility and any family which does not care for such members is regarded with disapproval. On the other hand, this sense of responsibility can have its drawbacks, for a family can be burdened with hangers-on who expect to be maintained, however small the family resources.

In times of rapid social change like the present, the extended family tends to disintegrate. This is the situation in many of the developing countries today. Industrialisation provides more opportunities in the towns and so the young people from the villages leave home to try their luck in a neighbouring city. For a time they keep up with their relatives but communications may become difficult, especially for a young family with children, and visits to their home in the country tend to drop off. The result is that the extended family breaks up and some of its branches are lost.

The nuclear family is more typical of urban, Western countries. It means a household, usually of two generations, consisting in most cases of parents with their children and perhaps an elderly grandparent. But this does not mean that such families are completely cut off from their more extended kin. Contemporary studies, like those of the Institute of Community Studies, show that some families in this country maintain contact with a very wide range of relatives and that holidays are often spent visiting them. Since in this country most married people regard themselves as members of two families – their own and that of their 'in-laws' – this could include quite a number of people.

Relationships within the extended family in other countries are rather different from those within a family here. In the former case, all relatives expect to be consulted about important decisions such as a marriage or a family move. Here, most family decisions are taken by the parents with the agreement perhaps of the older children and the grandparents. But other relatives are excluded. This means that such relatives in their turn do not expect to take much responsibility in family matters. They keep in touch spasmodically but do very little more, unless they happen to have some special attachment to the family such as being a godparent.

Since there is little sense of family solidarity, the nuclear family has a fragility which can cause great distress to its members. If a husband and wife fall out they may find little consolation or comfort within the family itself, and this may lead to a family break-up. The sufferers will be the children, who may not be wanted by either parent, and who may have to be cared for by the State. Such a situation would not arise in an extended family, where such children would automatically find a home with another relative.

Furthermore, since the nuclear family contains no large, close-knit groupings that can offer emotional and material help, it has no inbuilt way of taking care of the sick, the disabled and the elderly. Some families may manage to do so, but the smallness of many houses and the fact that both husband and wife have full-time jobs, may make this impossible. Such care has to be provided by the State social services, supported by the many and varied voluntary organisations which exist in this country for the purpose.

Society, Culture and Social Class

Though the extended family is rarely to be found in this country, social networks are fairly strong. These are the social contacts which people have, not only within the home, but with others outside it. They will know people in the neighbourhood where they live, the place where they work, the clubs to which they belong, the church they attend or among the friends they have made in one way or another. Everybody has a wide range of social contacts which, if traced, would tend to form a network over quite a large area.

Such social contacts involve people in a variety of different groupings of varying size and complexity, the widest of them being that of 'society'. So far the term 'society' has been used in a rather general way to indicate possible social contacts. It is now necessary to be more precise about what the term means. A simple way to decide whether a cluster of people qualifies as a society is to imagine that all other groupings except this one were suddenly to disappear. If there is a good chance that the surviving group would continue very much in its present form, then it qualifies as a 'society', since it is more or less complete in itself.

It is only when a group of people have clearly defined characteristics and keep themselves separate from the rest of the community that they can be regarded as a society. This is obviously the case with a primitive tribe, and another example is the Mennonites, who came to Pennsylvania, USA, from Germany a century or so ago, bringing with them a highly puritanical way of life. They are simple in dress and habits and disapprove of marriage outside the group. The families in this community produce almost everything they need, so there is little contact with the outside world. The musical *Plain and Fancy* made them familiar to people in Britain.

It is more difficult to distinguish a society in a country like ours where social contacts are highly complicated and interlinked. Those who follow a way of life of their own, like professional criminals and street corner gangs, could be regarded as such. But for most of us, society is the milieu in which we live, and is not at all clearly defined.

The importance of society is that its members have common patterns of behaviour, generally called 'culture'. This influences not only how they react to one another, but also the whole character and form of their homes. Thus a description of the culture of a London suburb would have to include such things as the daily routine of the inhabitants, their level of material possessions, the kind of house they live in, the clothes they wear, the amusements they enjoy and the decor of their homes. Their culture would be influenced not only by the level of technology reached in that society, but also by the values they hold, which means the ideas and attitudes they have about life in general.

All societies have their own particular culture, and although there may be some similarities, each is unique. This is obvious when there are differences in outside things, like language and behaviour, but less noticeable when values differ. Hence difficulties arise with immigrant families, like those from the West Indies, who are able to speak English, but who can mean very different things by the words they use and may have very different ideas about the forms of behaviour acceptable in this country.

Not only does each society have its own form of culture, it may also have within it sub-cultures, each with its different ways of behaving or sets of norms. For example, within British Society, isolated rural settlements such as those of the Hebrides have their own way of life which differs greatly from life in a big city. People in a wealthy suburb will live very differently from people in a densely populated down-town area. Young people at a pop festival will shock many of the families in the neighbourhood where they have chosen to hold their festival.

Social class is one of the most important determining factors of a sub-culture. Class divisions relate to society's tendency to rank people according to characteristics it regards as desirable. They include such things as wealth, education, suitable social contacts, types of occupation and leisure activities and lead to distinctions between the upper, middle and lower classes.

The upper class are usually people with money and property, who can trace their ancestry a long way back to a similar class, who have been to the older public schools and Oxford or Cambridge and who have similar sorts of friends. The middle class are reasonably well-to-do, tend to be employed in the professions or similar occupations, and usually want private schooling for their children and private medical treatment. The lower classes include the lower income groups who are employed in the less skilled levels of industry and commerce and have their own characteristic ways of living and behaving. The distinctions between classes are by no means watertight, for class boundaries are not very clearly defined and opinions differ greatly about which class a particular person belongs to. Nevertheless, in a society like ours, a great deal of what a person does, how he behaves, what chances he has in life, how he spends his leisure and so on is directly related to the social class to which he belongs.

The link between class and way of life is clearly brought out by Dennis Chapman in his book *The Home and Social Status*. Here he shows how class affects the type of house a family occupies, the way in which rooms are allocated for different purposes and between the members of the family, the furnishing and decorating of the rooms, the hours of meals and the food that is provided. For instance, the upper classes tend to live in detached houses which they own, and which have more than one living room. They usually have their main meal in the evening, while people in other social classes may not.

Social class had a far greater effect upon the family in the past than it does today. In fact, in the past, the way in which families lived was governed almost entirely by the conditions of the social class to which they belonged. Before the social upheavals of the nineteenth century, which resulted from the tremendous developments in industry and commerce that we call the industrial revolution, it was possible to distinguish two large and exclusive social classes, the nobility and the labourers, with a very small group of middle class families in between. They lived, dressed and spoke differently, so that there was never any doubt about which social class a person belonged to.

The nobility were usually very wealthy and owned vast amounts of property. Their main aim was to ensure that this property was handed on intact to an heir in the family. Therefore family life was centred on producing a suitable heir. Marriages were often arranged with this in mind, and families were large in order to ensure that if the eldest son died there would be others to fill his place. The heir was expected to supervise the management of the estates, and the other sons were found positions in established professions like the army, the navy, the Church, the legal profession or the diplomatic service. The daughters, as they grew up, were found suitable husbands within their own social class. Each, when she married, set up her own nuclear family, although the household, which consisted of innumerable servants and employees on the estate, could be quite large. But they all kept in very close touch with their relatives, and in this sense can be regarded as an example of the extended family.

The labourers worked on the land and were paid very little, on the grounds that much of what they needed was supplied by the landowner. The result was that they lived in very poor conditions, usually a small cottage, one room up and one down, with space only for the immediate family. They rarely left their villages, except on market days when they might go to the nearest town. So if their relatives happened to live in the same village or close by, they could keep in touch, but if they did not, very little family contact was maintained.

Those between the two large social classes included a small number of freeholders who owned their own farms, among them the parson. There were also those who went to work as domestic servants in the big houses, and so because somewhat isolated from their families in the village. The servants' hall had a life of its own, providing much better food and lodging than the labourer's cottage from which most of them came.

Class distinctions in the towns were not so apparent, largely because people on the whole were more well-to-do and some schooling was available. Many of the townsfolk were craftsmen earning a reasonable living, so they could send their children to the local school and set them up in business. Because most of these families remained in the town where they were born, their family life was close. Those who were more successful would become traders or merchants and it was from such families that leading citizens like the mayor were chosen.

The industrial revolution of the late eighteenth and early nineteenth centuries brought about a big change in social classes. Although the nobility still owned most of the land, their younger sons might now go into trade. At the same time, successful industrialists could buy up some of the big estates and after a generation or so become socially acceptable to the nobility. In this way they managed to breach the carefully guarded ranks of the upper class.

Working people, on the other hand, benefited very little from the industrial revolution. Many of them had to move into the towns to find work in the factories, and this usually meant that they were cut off from other members of the family who remained in the country. Living conditions in the towns were appalling, and since men, women and children all had to go out to work to earn enough to survive, it was very difficult to keep the home neat and tidy. The wife was often too tired to prepare meals or to attend to the needs of her husband and children.

With industrialisation came a new type of family – that of the middle class. These people were factory owners and those engaged in commerce, banking and other such occupations needed to support the great development in trade. They enjoyed a considerable amount of wealth, social status and influence. Changes in the franchise gave them power and a position in local government, and improvements in transport meant that they no longer had to live near the factory or the family business. They could therefore set up homes for themselves in the more pleasant suburbs. The wife was no longer required to take part in her husband's work, and since increasing wealth made domestic servants possible, she had very little to do in the home. Instead she led a busy social life, entertaining friends and neighbours and developing an interest in arts and crafts, music, sewing and embroidery. Many still existing Victorian charities, like the YWCA and Dr Barnardo's homes, date from this time, as helping the less privileged became a way of spending time for those who were not interested in entertaining.

A change came with the 1914–18 war, when most women helped in the war effort, either in the munition factories or voluntarily. Girls growing up in the 1920s expected to follow a career rather than stay at home until they found a husband. The 1939–45 war brought a far greater change, for those who had previously gone into domestic service could now find employment in the many personal services demanded, such as catering, hairdressing and office work. As a result, servants became very scarce and expensive, so that the middle class mother now had to look after her own children, cook for the family and do much of the housework.

Working people, on the other hand, began to earn far higher wages than they had done in the past and so could buy many of the things which had previously been restricted to middle class families. They were able to buy similar clothes, furnish their homes in a similar way, eat very much the same sorts of food, own a car, and go for holidays abroad. Class distinctions are not nearly so apparent now. But this does not mean that they are not here. They are present in more subtle ways, such as in the priorities in expenditure on things like education and private medicine, and in the forms that entertaining and holidays may take.

The Contemporary British Family

The result of this change is that for the first time in generations it is possible to define a type of family which is fairly uniform throughout Britain. The family is now small. This is the result of an increasing number of parents deciding to restrict the size of their family. Middle class parents in the later years of the nineteenth century were the first to do this, largely because they were doubtful whether the prosperity they had experienced for a generation or so was going to last. At first family size was reduced by putting marriage off for several years with the result that the woman had fewer years in which she could become pregnant. Then greater publicity about birth control led to its being more widely practised. As the standard of living of working people rose and their education improved, they too began to take an interest in birth control, so that by the time of the period between the two world wars both middle and working class families were greatly reduced in size. The Royal Commission on Population, reporting in 1949, put the average family as 2·2 children. For a decade or so after this, the figure rose slightly, but in the last decade families have been gradually shrinking in size, and the number of children entering school is falling.

The family is also tending to remain in existence for a longer time. This is partly due to the fact that people are marrying younger because of the comparative well-being of our society, which increasingly enables young people to earn an adequate income and so to secure somewhere to live. In 1921 the average age of marriage for men was 27 and for women 25. It is now 24 and 22 respectively. Many more men are marrying under the age of 21 and a large number of women are under eighteen when they marry.

At the other extreme people tend to live longer. This is due to advances in medical care and to the reduction of poverty and malnutrition. Women at the age of 40 can expect another 37 years of life, and men at the same age another 32 years. This gives the average man and woman some fifty years of married life together, of which only about a third is occupied with bringing up the family. Most mothers have a child within the first two years of married life and so their children may have left school by the time they are 40. This leaves them with some twenty years of comparative freedom in which they can either return to work or find some alternative occupation.

Most couples are able to afford their own home on marriage, though the housing situation in some areas may make this difficult. Once a family has acquired a home of its own it tends to keep this home intact, though it may not always occupy the same premises. A family moves on an average three or four times in its existence, but it usually continues to occupy the family home until one of the parents dies. By this time the children will have left home, and so the remaining parent will frequently go to live with one of the children.

These characteristics of the small, longer-lived family with a home of its own tend to keep the nuclear family in existence. Parents, children and grandchildren are in close touch with one another, but other relatives are not so important. Again there are differences between the classes. While the middle class on the whole keep their relatives at a distance and only call upon them in urgent need, working class people have a far closer family relationship, especially if their relatives live fairly close at hand. Moving to a new town or council estate can adversely affect this sort of relationship. Thus it is mostly among immigrants that the extended form of family is still to be found.

Within the family itself, the roles of the sexes are becoming far less distinct. In the past, the husband was expected to exercise the control while the wife cared for the home and the children. There was a fairly rigid division of labour in the home and children were expected to 'be seen and not heard'. Now husband and wife are much more likely to share the tasks of the home and children are more free to do what they like and to express their own opinions. Young and Willmott draw attention to this in their book *The Symmetrical Family*. They describe the contemporary family as based on companionship, with its members far more equal in their roles. But they still find a place for some differences in the functions and the performance of the sexes. There are some jobs that the mother can do better and others, especially those that require physical strength, like digging the garden, which are usually left to the man.

Family life tends to be much more home-centred than was the case in the past, especially when the children are young. This has happened in the middle class because there are no longer servants to look after the children or to help in the house. On the other hand, working class people now have homes which are far more comfortable and warm and so outside attractions are relatively less strong. Television keeps the family together in all the income groups, and ownership of a car means that they go out together on day excursions and holidays.

The attitude of parents to children has also changed. In the past the welfare of the child was secondary to that of the parents. Children were punished severely if they did not do what was expected of them. They had to conform closely to the social customs of the group to which they belonged. Now the child is all-important and his or her requirements are given priority, even if they do not fit in with what other children in the family circle are doing.

Improvements in preventive medicine have also made a difference to the modern family. In the past the family could do little more than help to ease the sufferings of the sick child. Modern drugs, especially those used for immunisation, make childhood illnesses less prevalent and not nearly so dangerous as they used to be. Parents are able to afford medical care for their children now that most of the medical and health services are free and available to all.

There are two important factors behind these changes in the structure and life of the family. One of them is the growth of feminism. The changing attitude to women means that they are accepted in their own right, find employment in most occupations on a level with men, and have to be paid and treated similarly. This is reflected in the home. The husband and wife now have reciprocal rights and duties and their partnership is a more equal one.

The other factor which has permitted these changes is modern technological development which has been applied to equipment in the home. At first such technology was concentrated on the needs of industry. It is now used to a great extent to make labour-saving equipment for the home. The rise in family incomes, especially in the lower classes of society, has created a large market for such equipment. Few families are now without a vacuum cleaner or an electric iron, and many have a dishwasher and a freezer.

Immigrant Families
So far we have been concerned with the typical native British family. But our society contains an increasing number of families from overseas. This is not new. The Huguenots came to Britain from France to escape persecution in the sixteenth century, and many other groups like the Jews have taken refuge in this country from time to time, and been integrated with the local population. There are differences, however, between these earlier immigrants and those who have come in recent years. Many of the immigrants who have come since the 1950s are from sub-tropical areas like India, Pakistan, the West Indies and Central Africa. Their background and their cultures are very different from those of immigrants who came from Europe, and very many of them are from new Commonwealth countries.

These new immigrants come from societies which believe in the extended family, and they find our family relationships difficult to understand. They bring with them their own native culture which can be very different from the British way of life. Religious customs and rituals play a far more important part in their lives than they do in ours, and often influence their behaviour. This may involve food taboos, such as not eating pork, and dress taboos, such as not going bareheaded. Such taboos can conflict with the normal practice in this country, and a great deal of trouble can be caused by lack of understanding. Sikhs, for instance, found themselves in difficulties over the compulsory wearing of crash helmets, because their religion requires the men to wear a turban. (The law has since been amended in their favour.)

Language is another problem. Many immigrants are unfamiliar with English and cannot communicate easily with other people. The children may not do well at school because the methods of learning are new to them, and many of the men can only do unskilled jobs because more complicated work requires a greater knowledge of English than they have. The women have similar problems. Until they learn English they can remain isolated in their homes, unable to cope with the outside world.

But perhaps the biggest problem is that of values. The Asians, in particular, believe that British society is morally decadent. They regard our dress as immodest and the normal free behaviour of British women as provocative. They are dismayed by the lack of respect that some British children show to their parents, and by the failure of adults to care for elderly relatives, especially parents. They are shocked by the ease with which marriages break up, and the number of divorces which take place. So they exercise strong discipline in the home, especially with teenagers, and try to shield them from what they regard as the corrupting influences around them. The young people become frustrated, for they cannot ask their friends home, and they are not allowed to go out with them.

With the second generation of immigrants the problems have changed. They have been educated here, and they speak the language. They have had an opportunity of finding a reasonable job and they understand something of the British way of life. They now behave in an Anglicised way at work, but at the same time they want to keep their own customs and traditions. In some ways the tensions of living have increased. They are now able to mix with British people more easily, but they find they are not wanted as close friends or neighbours. Yet the ties with their own countryfolk have begun to loosen. They seem to themselves to be between two cultures. Only time will tell whether these families will become fully assimilated and accepted into British society.

The big change that has affected both British and immigrant families in this country is that instead of being producing units, they are now consumers. When families were relatively poor, as British families were in the nineteenth century, and as immigrant families are now in their own countries, they had to spend all their energies in earning a living. This they did in the factories and the fields producing the goods that were put on the market. The family of the late twentieth century has a far higher income, which it can spend on a variety of consumer goods which are not necessarily essentials of life. The family can have a varied diet; it can buy more or less what it wants to furnish or equip the home; and it has something left over for pleasure. The family has become a consuming unit. Together its members plan their expenditure on commodities which will enhance the comfort and well-being of the home. How they do this is discussed in Chapter 3. Meanwhile we must look more closely at personal relationships within the family.

2 The Family Group

One important feature of the family is that it consists of a group of people who are brought together, through no choice of their own, into an intimate relationship with one another. They know one another well, are aware of one another's likes and dislikes, and often know in advance how another member of the family is likely to respond to them. This relationship starts at birth when the infant first becomes aware of other people. It continues throughout childhood and adolescence, when the people closest are parents, brothers and sisters. A new relationship is formed with marriage, and this relationship changes as the children are born and grow up. By this time another family has come into being, with its own special types of relationships.

Personal Relationships
Wherever we go we are constantly forming relationships with other people. We form a relationship with the shop assistant when we go to buy clothes. If we ask the way when we are lost, a relationship is formed with the person who directs us. Relationships are formed at school, at work and in the many other groups of people with whom we mix. However self-sufficient we may be, the society in which we live makes it necessary for us to be continually making relationships of one sort or another if we are to survive.

These relationships vary in type depending upon the group in which they take place. It is usual to distinguish between primary groups, in which relationships are close, and secondary groups, where they are more remote and ill-defined. In a primary group the members meet one another face to face and know one another fairly intimately. They are concerned with one another's affairs. These are often called small interest groups; they are of a size and type in which relationships can be reasonably intimate; and they are more or less permanent in duration so that relationships tend to be fairly deep.

The most important primary groups in which people find themselves are the family and the neighbourhood or village in which they live. In both cases they have generally become part of the group through circumstances outside their own control. People are born into a family and have no choice at all in the matter. They live in a particular village or form part of a neighbourhood in a town usually to be near their places of work, or because they have been allocated accommodation there by the local authority. It will not necessarily be the place they would choose to live in, but some special circumstances have placed them there. Once they have come to live in a place, they become involved in the numerous relationships which it demands.

Yet people have a certain amount of choice in the relationships which they form with other people in their village or neighbourhood. Mothers taking their children to school will get to know other mothers, but they can choose which ones they will get to know well. A person may decide to join a group such as the Scouts, the British Legion or the local Church, but he does not have to do so and he is usually free to leave at any time. Quite often people will join groups like these when their outside relationships are restricted, for example when their children are young or when they have retired from work and need some outside interests.

Some families form very close relationships with their neighbours and these relationships will be primary in character. This usually happens if they have something in common, such as children of a similar age, or some shared interest like gardening. On the other hand there may be no desire or need for such a relationship and neighbours may have merely a nodding acquaintance. When this is so, their relationship would be classed as secondary.

Many secondary relationships are formed for some specific purpose and when that purpose no longer exists the relationship ceases. For example, a pressure group may be formed by parents who come together to demand a pedestrian crossing on a main road so that their children can go to school in safety. Relationships of a sort will be formed when the members of the group are dealing with the local council over the matter or planning a demonstration. But they are not likely to be very deep, or to last once the purpose has been achieved.

What really matters for most people are the relationships in the family group. The family offers security and stability, which are not often found in the more formalised, impersonalised relationships which exist in most other groups. It provides a more or less permanent relationship regardless of the ups and downs through which most relationships pass, and it possesses a certain amount of control over what its members do and how they behave. The result is that reasonably happy relationships can usually be maintained.

In the past, control over family relationships was fairly well defined because there were traditional patterns for the establishment, development and breakdown of the family. Some of these are described in the anthropological studies of Margaret Mead, such as *Male and Female* and *Coming of Age in Samoa*. But in our contemporary society, although we do have accustomed patterns for marriage, bringing up our children and getting separated or divorced, conformity to these patterns is not very strict. The patterns tend to change so fast that what one generation takes for granted, like seeking one's parents' permission to marry, the next generation will reject. Nevertheless, it is possible to arrive at some idea of the usual ways in which a family gets established and continues to function.

The Establishment of a Family
Dating, courtship and marriage precede the establishment of a family and social customs have played a large part in these in the past. There used to be traditional ways of doing these things which were followed very closely. In a few societies such as the rural areas of the Near East, India and Pakistan, the choice of a marriage partner is often still made by relatives. They will take into account such things as the personalities of the two young people, whether they appear to be compatible, the social groups from which they come and the social status of their parents. Soothsayers may be brought in to assess the characters of the two people, horoscopes may be consulted and health and family connections carefully weighed up. This is still done in some first-generation immigrant families, much to the distress of the young people concerned.

Until comparatively recently, parents in this country exercised a fairly rigid control over the choice of friends their adolescent children made. Young people were expected to choose their friends from neighbouring families or from those with whom their parents were acquainted. Parents decided whom their children met and what time they spent with their friends. They were expected to tell their parents where they were going and to be home by a certain time. Only when an engagement was announced were young people allowed comparative freedom in their relationships.

Most families now leave the young person relatively free to select a mate. So the dating relationship has become important as a way in which to select and test out a prospective marriage partner. Dating usually starts at the beginning of puberty as a way of getting to know the opposite sex. It is an educational process in which each learns about the other, and in so doing develops a knowledge and understanding of sex relationships. Since changes in dating-partners are frequent, it is possible to discover a great deal about the opposite sex before marriage, and one of our moral problems today is the limit to which this relationship should be carried.

Dating with the same person for a period of time, or 'going steady', usually leads to an engagement. In the past engagements were fairly long because it was frequently necessary to save money for a year or so in order to set up a home. Now engagements can be very short indeed, because most young people are earning enough to do this at very short notice. Nor do most couples seek the permission of their parents before entering into an official engagement. But the Family Law Reform Act, 1969, makes it necessary for persons under the age of eighteen to obtain the consent of their parents before marriage, and no one can enter into a contract of marriage under the age of sixteen.

In spite of these departures from traditional customs, studies have shown that the pattern of courting has not changed as much as might be expected. Although young people who live at home are usually free to go out with whom they wish, and those who live on their own in a city or study at a university or college have a very wide choice of mate, they still marry within fairly restricted areas. A large proportion of weddings still take place between people living relatively close to one another, and between people of a similar social class and background. This is perhaps what one would expect, since people are usually drawn together by common interests.

There are still problems of so-called 'mixed marriages'. These take place between people of different race, ethnic group, or religious background, for example the marriage of a white to a coloured person, a Jew to a Christian or a Roman Catholic to a Protestant. In the past, the groups concerned have greatly discouraged this. But today there is far greater freedom for such marriages, though they may mean that the people concerned are cut off from their families and suffer a certain amount of isolation as a consequence. Much of the harm is experienced by the children of such a marriage who may be unacceptable to both groups. This happens more often when the mixed marriage is one of colour, because there is still a certain amount of prejudice against such marriages.

Most marriage partners in modern society choose each other freely as people, on the grounds of 'being in love'. Their marriage relationship starts with a romantic involvement, which is regarded as mutual and between partners with equal rights. Both expect to have an equal share in taking decisions, pooling resources and following their individual tastes and interests.

These factors can cause difficulties in the marriage relationship. Mutual attraction is not always lasting and its character tends to change with time. It is then that common interests and tastes become the binding factor, so that when these are lacking the marriage may flounder. One partner may seek someone else who seems more attractive; or one partner may try to dominate the other.

Thus the relationship between a husband and a wife in modern society becomes an extremely delicate affair. The successful working out of this relationship and its problems depends very much upon continuous and individual effort on the part of both partners. It calls for much personal adjustment and mutual consideration, which has to be made continuously. Today husbands and wives have to work out their own relationships in the particular circumstances in which they find themselves, with very little help from other people and no traditional pattern to which they can refer. This is no easy matter.

Many couples prefer simply to live together rather than to enter into a contract of marriage. This places an even greater burden on mutual attraction and agreement, but makes it easier for the two people to part if necessary. But when two people have lived together for a time, parting always causes some distress. Therefore many people think that getting married and being bound by a marriage contract is better than living together, because it always delays a breakdown of the relationship and so gives time for reconsideration.

Children, their Development and Care
Marriage usually leads to children and many women have a child within the first two years of marriage. Now that family planning is far more reliable, and advice and treatment can be obtained under the National Health Service, it is possible to regulate the size and spacing of a family. It is also possible to put off starting a family for a while after marriage to enable a wife to continue her career, or to support a husband who is still engaged in further education or training for a job. This relieves the partners of much worry with regard to unwanted pregnancies. It also makes it possible for them to have a family when they want to and bring the children up with greater care and devotion.

Most parents are concerned about the growth and development of their children. They want them to have at least the advantages which they themselves had, and many parents want better things for their children. They are therefore interested in any suggestions they may hear or read about on the bringing up and care of children.

The difficulty in studying the development of the child is that all children are different and so what can be said about one child may not refer so well to another. It is therefore necessary to deal in generalisations and to modify these for a particular child.

Physical health and growth are obviously very important to the development of the child. Other aspects of growth which need to be considered are: the development of intelligence and the capacity for learning which become apparent when the child reaches school age; emotional development, which can often be discovered only when the child differs from other children either by excessively aggressive behaviour or by withdrawal from others; social development, which is indicated by the extent to which the child finds it easy to mix with other playmates and to get on at home; and moral or personality development, which takes place very gradually.

Many books on child development concentrate on one or other of these aspects instead of on the child as a whole, and this gives an unbalanced approach to the subject. Since the various developments occur at different times in a child's life, the best way to look at them, and to include them all, is to define the various stages through which children pass and discuss the developments at each stage, at the same time showing how parents, through their care of the child, can help to meet the problems and difficulties presented at each stage.

We learn from Dr John Bowlby's well-known book, *Child Care and the Growth of Love,* that it is the first five years of a child's life that are of the greatest importance. It is during this time that basic attitudes and ways of dealing with the emotions are formed. It is therefore essential during these years that the child should feel secure and happy whatever happens, since if he can approach the early years of life in this way, he is likely to be able to meet the problems of later years in a similar manner. The worst possible thing is for the young child to feel isolated, hungry, lonely and helpless, for a child deprived in this way in babyhood may feel deprived and insecure for the rest of his life.

At first the child is closest to his mother and the initial bond is that of feeding. Opinions differ as to the comparative advantages of breast and bottle feeding. But there is little doubt that disturbed feeding and unsuitable feeding can have far-reaching psychological and physical results. Therefore great attention needs to be paid to the sort of food which is suitable for the particular child and to the way in which it is given.

Food can easily become an emotional issue, especially during weaning. This is because weaning is the first step a child takes towards independence, and a mishandling of this situation can cause a fear of rejection and desertion which may last throughout life. Sudden or abrupt weaning, and foods which the child does not like, not only cause fear in the child but also arouse anxiety or annoyance in the mother which is easily conveyed to the child. To try to ease this situation, the child today is given new foods and tastes at a very early age and so is gradually accustomed to changes in diet.

Toilet training has very similar effects if it is harshly or hurriedly carried out. Emotion or anxiety on the part of the mother can easily be transferred to the child. John and Elizabeth Newson comment more fully on these matters in their book *Patterns of Infant Care in an Urban Community.*

The infant feels sensations, such as hot and cold, hard and soft, pleasant and unpleasant, very keenly, so that he soon learns that certain qualities belong to certain things and that certain results will follow certain actions. At first positive movements are almost entirely automatic, but gradually the child learns to deal with his own problems.

He learns to get a spoon to his mouth instead of being fed, and to crawl around on the floor instead of staying in his cot or pram. Learning to talk follows later and is very much a matter of imitation. The child whose mother is constantly talking to him may learn much sooner than the child whose mother takes little notice of him. This is a reason for slowness of speech in children who are brought up in a children's home.

The speed of development of children is very variable. Children are individuals and develop at their own rate. But there are reasons for very slow development. This may be because the child is delicate or has some illness. There may be some disturbance in early life such as a change of home if the parents are on the move, or if the child is in the care of foster parents and these have to be changed. The child who is continually surrounded by quarrelling or is afraid that one parent may leave home permanently, is in a particularly insecure and threatened position.

During the pre-school period there is an increase in muscular control and the child gradually develops the mastery of his limbs. He walks and runs, climbs and balances, and smaller muscles begin to be used. Hence he feels a need to do simple things for himself, such as dressing and washing his own hands and face. He can be given toys which encourage this development, such as threading beads or matching colours, and this will usually happen if the child goes to a play school or nursery. His vocabulary will increase and he will replace simple forms of speaking by more complicated sentences. Again stimulation from adults and the cultural level of the home will help.

Relationships with other members of the family gradually develop. At first the child needs to achieve a happy, easy, natural relationship with his parents. Psychology tells us that the young child, after his infancy period, will become attached emotionally to the parent of the opposite sex. This means that a boy tends to be more emotionally involved with his mother, while a girl becomes attached to her father. These relationships are satisfactory for a time, but the society in which we live demands that a boy must learn to behave like his father and a girl like her mother if they are to take their proper place in life. This means that a boy has to learn to change from being a son to becoming a husband and father, and a girl needs to know how to be a mother and organiser of the home. If this change does not take place satisfactorily the boy may be effeminate and the girl too masculine, and this can have an adverse effect upon their future marriage and home life. Fortunately, today there is far less distinction between the roles which the boy and the girl are expected to play in life, and so the importance of these changes is not so great.

Methods of child rearing may vary according to the country concerned and the fashion of the moment. Sometimes very strong disciplinary control is exercised which involves various forms of punishment. This was typical of Britain in Victorian times, when the old tradition of 'spare the rod and spoil the child' was followed. Victorian novels illustrate this attitude. But in the 1920s psychologists taught that heavy punishment inflicted on a child could have lasting bad effects upon his behaviour as an adult. They advocated the need for children to be allowed to develop with the least possible restraint.

The result has been a more understanding and a more permissive attitude towards the behaviour of children. Parents try to understand why children do not do as they are told, rather than force them to obey. Of course, this can go too far when children are allowed to do exactly as they like, causing annoyance and disturbance among the people with whom they live. But if followed in moderation, this attitude can mean greater happiness to all members of the family. The actual details of child rearing vary from one generation to another, but today they are based on what is learnt at the local health centre, as well as what is read in women's magazines.

As the child grows up, the parents need to loosen their control gradually and help him to become more independent. This means helping him to stand on his own feet so that he can leave the security of the family environment and forge ahead himself. In many societies, particularly primitive ones, there are ceremonies which mark this change in status from childhood to adolescence. The child leaves home for a time to be initiated into the ways of adult behaviour, and when he comes back he is regarded by everyone as a grown-up. This means that both the child and the adults realise a change that has taken place and are ready to make the necessary adjustment. The change in status is quite often made visible by some physical mark like tattooing or by adult clothes and the bearing of arms.

In Western society children are helped to grow up by association with groups of boys or girls of their own age – often known as peer groups. They begin to choose friends outside their own families, of the same sex as themselves. In doing this they form close and intimate groups which often take on the nature of a secret society. In these groups they may use a special language which others cannot understand, they may have their own ways of behaving and of communicating with one another, and they learn from one another what the larger society to which they now belong demands. In other words they learn to grow up.

When they reach adolescence they have noticeable physiological changes to deal with as well. These can have a disturbing effect on the young person, and are often accompanied by emotional difficulties such as sharp swings in mood and irritability. The young person may scrutinise and criticise his parents, flout their opinions, disregard their authority, challenge their beliefs and look to his companions for support in this. The trouble is that the role of parenthood combines both intimacy and authority. As the adolescent passes into adulthood he tries to loose the ties of intimacy with parents in favour of the opposite sex of his own age group, and he flaunts the authority of adults since he himself is becoming one. The tensions which result are severe, because in our modern society there are no recognised steps by which authority can be relinquished gradually and adjustment made in the various areas of intimacy.

The basic difficulty in Western society is that the maturity of physical growth does not correspond with admission to adult ways of life. It is some years after the beginning of physical maturity before the adolescent is regarded as a true adult and permitted to behave as one. He is not expected to participate in adult sexual or economic roles until well after the time he has reached physical adulthood. There is therefore a period during which he feels like, and expects to be regarded as, an adult, and yet is very rarely regarded as such.

It is during this period too that most young people pass from school to work and have to make adjustments in this sphere as well. They may have to take a job in which they are not really interested, or if they stay in their home town they may fail to find employment. On the other hand, if they move away they have to find somewhere to live in an unfamiliar place, and to face the difficulties of new surroundings as well as those of a first job. Whatever choice they make, they will have to work far longer hours than they are used to, adapt themselves to commuting and live more independently.

The rapid social changes in society today accentuate these adjustments. Neither parents nor young people are sure of the course they should follow. Parents feel that they should be somewhat more restrictive in what they allow their young people to do, and young people themselves want more freedom than their parents are willing to give. There is no authority in our modern society which has power to act as an adjudicator.

So in most Western countries there is what is termed 'adolescent rebellion'. This is nothing new, of course. But adolescents today seem more turbulent than ever before. They have created for themselves their own form of culture and behaviour which is very different from life as most adults know it. This is seen not only in clothes and general behaviour, but in different values and attitudes, and it is the latter that cause much of the trouble. Some young people tend to be more permissive in their attitude to sex than the older generation can tolerate. They are trying out ideas which hardly occurred to the previous generation. Some young people prefer a communal to a family way of living. They may take over a large country house, share it out among several families in their own age range, work on the land or at some handicraft, and have meals and care for the children as a group.

On the other hand, many modern young people bring to life a directness and a search for truth which the previous generation did not even consider. They put this into practice by seeking freedom and justice for the underprivileged on a far wider scale than has been done in the past. They form their own societies to help those in need and do this on a personal basis, living among the people who need their help and giving them the advice and support they require. Groups like Release, which helps drug addicts and drop-outs, are an example.

The result is that methods of child rearing today have not only to deal with the ordinary adjustments that take place in the development of the young. They also have to take account of the tremendous social changes that have been happening in recent decades. Parents in the past could call on their own childhood experiences for guidance, but today their values and attitudes have little place in the outlook of their children. Child rearing has therefore become less a matter of following a given pattern, and more of a trial and error exercise in adapting to the new forms our culture is taking. It is therefore hardly surprising that at times it seems as though there is very little method or thought in what is being done.

Relationships within the Family
Within the family there are a variety of people of different ages, personality and aims in life. There may be just the parents and children. Sometimes there is a grandparent. Other relatives, like uncles, aunts and cousins, usually come and go, though most of them will arrive for special occasions like birthdays, weddings, funerals and baptisms. They often have much to say about the other members of the family and may try to influence family policy.

Relationships between these people are not always easy, though they may be better with some members of the family than with others. Basically relationships are a matter of personality. Some personalities complement each other and so get on well together. If one person is irritable, the other is able to smooth things over. On the other hand, personalities may clash. If one person is angry, the other may be even more furious, and a real row will take place.

Personality is to a large extent a matter of inheritance and so members of a family may be very similar. This can lead to serious family quarrels which are very difficult to resolve. It is here that in-laws can often help, since they are likely to have personalities of a different type and may be able to intervene, without emotion, in a difficult situation.

Members of a family are also faced with the problem of the many different roles they are expected to play. Thus the man will have to be a husband to his wife, a father to his children and a son to his own mother. Each of these roles requires a different sort of relationship, and if the people involved are all living together constant changes of role will be necessary. The role of the child is less complicated than that of the adult since he is always in the position of a child, although his relationship with his parents may be different from that with other relatives. Even he is aware of these differences in role, for one of the most absorbing games children play, is dressing up and pretending to be mothers and fathers.

The happiness of a family with young children depends very much on how the children get on with one another. Family size and the spacing of children are important in this regard. In a large family an older brother or sister can often give a younger one support when things are difficult, and the young child has someone to copy when he is not quite sure how to behave. This is most effective when age differences are small. It is here that an only child suffers. He has no one in whom to confide and the only people he can copy are his parents. The parents, too, suffer from having the child with them all the time. Therefore, if they are wise, they will arrange for some companionship of the same age for their child, either by sending him to nursery school or inviting other children to stay during the school holidays.

Difficulties may arise when a child who is not a relative, like a foster child or an adopted child, is introduced into the family. There may not be a personality clash, for an acceptable personality and background are important factors in matching the family with the child. But there are likely to be problems of adjustment. The child may not live up to the great expectations the family had of him, and he himself may find things difficult. Very careful preparation of all the members of a family is needed before the child arrives, and this has to be followed up with watchfulness on the part of the parents if relationships are to be successful.

Relationships between members of a family can change throughout life. Sometimes they will be good; at other times there may be great differences of opinion. This is because situations are never entirely the same. Children grow up and relationships with their parents change. The love of husband and wife will alter at different stages of their marriage, for example when some members of the family leave the home permanently. But there is a tendency for the family to come together again later on. A daughter may come back to live with her mother or brothers and sisters may live together when they are elderly. This is because their differences have mellowed with time and they find a certain security in their common background and the memory of things they shared as children.

Family relationships can be altered by a change in the composition of the family such as the arrival of a new baby, or the arrival of an elderly relative to live with the family. Similarly things like illness, a handicap or an accident can have profound repercussions on the family. They can alter relationships drastically and involve the family members in a sudden period of adjustment for which they are often quite unprepared.

When a new baby is coming, particularly a first child, relationships between husband and wife have to alter because the chief concern of the wife will now be for her child. Both parents will need to concentrate on making a home for the three of them so that each may feel he has his rightful place. The coming of later children may not be so difficult, because the family will by then have adjusted to two different generations and an additional member is more easily absorbed.

An elderly relative coming to live with a married son or daughter poses a similar problem, for it means the addition of another generation to the family. Quite often the youngest generation gets on well with the oldest, since grandparents are sufficiently distant from their grandchildren to be able to look at them in a fairly understanding and lenient way. They also have little responsibility for the children's behaviour, and so an intimate relationship may spring up between these generations. On the other hand, parents may resent the so-called interference of grandparents, and grandchildren may not like grandparents whose ways seem somewhat eccentric to them.

In an extended family, if an elderly relative does not get on with a family member there is usually some other relative with whom he or she can live. But in the small nuclear family, a difficult elderly relative has little choice. The family itself is faced with weighing up the priorities in meeting the responsibility of caring for the relative and putting other members of the family, usually the children, first. In most cases it is the children who take priority and the elderly relative has to go into a 'home'.

When a member of a family is born handicapped or becomes handicapped later in life through some crippling illness or accident, the effect upon family relationships can be disastrous. A handicap may be mental or physical and quite often a little of both. It may mean lack of sight, hearing or some impediment in bodily movement. It can even mean the lack of certain limbs or parts of the body (as in the case of thalydomide children), which can be very disfiguring, and distressing to other people. The problems involved are related to the degree of the handicap and the extent to which health and mobility are expected to deteriorate.

When a mother finds that her baby is handicapped it can cause her great distress, and it may be some time before she believes it. Usually this is a passing phase and she gradually accepts the fact. But there may be difficulties when the baby is taken home, particularly if it is disfigured in some way. On the other hand, if the child needs care, it may be treated as a kind of pet and given too much attention, while the other children suffer.

Therefore the most important thing the mother has to do is to get the family to treat the child as far as possible as normal. The extent to which this is possible will depend very much on the age of the other members of the family. When they are young it may be far easier, for they may be hardly aware of the handicap. But as they grow up it may become more difficult, as they will have to explain to their friends that they have a handicapped brother or sister. At this stage the mother has to weigh up the needs of the handicapped child against those of her other children and decide whether he should be looked after somewhere else for a time.

There are often special classes for the slightly handicapped child at an ordinary school, and if he is in hospital for any length of time, he may be taught there. If the child is unable to go to school, it may be possible for a teacher to come to the home and perhaps show the mother how to help her child to learn. For the severely handicapped child a special school is usually necessary. Most of these are residential because they cover a large area, and because the children may benefit from education in a boarding school where they can gradually learn to do things for themselves. The child may come home for weekends and during the school holidays, so that he does not lose touch with his family completely.

Many young people who are handicapped are capable of doing a job, but find it difficult to obtain one. Registers of disabled people are kept locally and the disablement settlement officer is responsible for assessing the ability of the person and finding him a suitable job. There are sheltered workshops like Remploy for the more severely disabled, where they are paid at the going rate, even though they may not be able to do as much work as a healthy person. Many of these workshops have a hostel so that the young person can live away from home and be as independent as possible.

In the past the handicapped young person usually had to give up any idea of marriage. But with the home aids now available, marriage is becoming possible. In fact, in some of the homes for handicapped people there are one or two flats for those who have married.

The parents of a handicapped child who is incapable of work and still lives at home face a very difficult situation. They are anxious not only about the present but about the future, when they will no longer be able to look after their son or daughter. Some can make arrangements for alternative care, but most of these young people will eventually have to go into a 'home'.

When one of the parents suddenly becomes handicapped through an accident or some incapacitating illness, changes are inevitable in family life. If it is the father who is affected, financial resources may be curtailed, and though State provision can help in various practical ways, much depends on the attitude of the person himself and the extent to which he can adapt to the new situation. Quite often the mother has to take over many of the family responsibilities as well as going out to work herself, so that the children may have to help with the cooking and cleaning.

If it is the mother who is incapacitated, the younger children may suffer, for she may find it difficult to care for them and exercise the authority that is needed. But in many such families as the children grow up they gain a sense of responsibility which is rarely found in the child from an ordinary home. When the incapacity is mental the mother will usually have to go away for a time until the children are old enough to understand the situation.

A handicap in one of the family members need not necessarily have a crippling effect upon family life. Some of the happiest families are in this situation. Adjustment is needed on the part of all the members of the family, and usually a doctor, social worker or clergyman can help with this. Some people find it far easier than others to alter their way of life and accept what has happened, in which case the family soon settles down to its changed circumstances.

The Single-Parent Family
Most families in this country consist of parents and children, each with his or her own special part to play in family life. But sometimes the family unit breaks up and only one parent remains. This may be due to natural causes like the death of one of the parents, or it may be the result of a breakdown in the relationship between husband and wife.

When one of the parents dies, the other parent is left to look after the children. If the mother dies, the father has to make arrangements for the care of the family while he is away at work. This may fall to the lot of the eldest in the family, who has this responsibility while still at school. Sometimes, when there are very young children, the father may have to give up his job and stay at home for a while, living on social security. But whatever the father decides to do, he will have much more housework to do, as well as the difficult task of bringing up the children on his own.

If it is the father who dies, the chief problem which faces the mother is a financial one. She is now dependent on the resources that have been left to her, and any help that the State may give. This can mean that she has to take a full-time job to support the family. This can affect the care of her children, although quite often they accept the extra responsibility they have to take and the family can be happy and well organised. The children are more likely to suffer from the lack of a father's control and the absence of an adult male at home.

Children may find it very difficult to deal with the problem of death, for it involves the loss of one who has always been very close to them, and whom they have never been without for any length of time. The remaining parent has the task of helping them to realise that they have not been abandoned, but that the way in which they are looked after has changed.

When the marriage relationship breaks down and a separation or divorce follows, the situation is different. There has probably been quite a long period of quarrelling and dissension in the home, with one or other of the parents absent from time to time. Thus the effect on the family is usually felt long before the break takes place. The inevitable sense of insecurity generated can communicate itself to the children with the result that their relationships at school or with their friends are already affected before their parents' separation.

Family breakdown of this nature is more common today than it was in the past. This is partly because separation and divorce have become much more acceptable in society, and divorce is now far easier. Under the Matrimonial Causes Act, 1973, the grounds for divorce have been changed from the committing of certain acts, like adultery or desertion, to the irretrievable breakdown of the marriage. If a marriage has gone so wrong that it appears quite impossible to restore it, the court can grant a divorce. The present position is that a divorce can be granted after two years of living apart if both parties request it, and after five years if only one of the parties wants it. But every endeavour has to be made to restore the relationship (and this includes agreeing to marriage counselling) before the court will give its consent.

Divorce also occurs more frequently today because under modern conditions of living the marriage relationship has become much more complicated. There are no longer separate and defined roles for husband and wife which complement each other. Most wives expect to go out to work, either part- or full-time, and so the husband has to share in the domestic tasks. He may have to do the shopping on a Saturday, or care for the children when his wife gets home late. What each partner does is determined largely by the prevailing circumstances – and they may disagree over the division of tasks. As well as this, the greater expectation of life means that they have many more years to live together and so longer to fall out.

All this makes the working out of a successful marital relationship a much more demanding and intricate affair than it has been hitherto. It has brought new stresses to the contemporary family where there are no longer the customary clear-cut patterns for each partner to follow. Instead the couple are left to solve their difficulties very much on their own, with perhaps the help of a marriage guidance counsellor or a social worker.

There are certain periods in a marriage when difficulties are more likely to occur. The first five years tend to be the most crucial ones, for during this time the two young people, often with varying personalities and backgrounds, are trying to adjust to each other. The next stage of marital difficulty will usually come when the children grow up and leave home. Instead of the home being centred on the children, the husband and wife have now to learn to live on their own again. Then, when retirement comes, they have to get used to spending most of each day together.

Various other circumstances can affect the marital relationship. For example, when housing is bad and there is little privacy, or it is difficult for the wife to keep the family and the home clean, problems may arise. Money troubles are frequently a cause of friction, either when there is not sufficient coming in or when one of the partners keeps a bigger share for himself or herself. Other relatives or 'in-laws' may interfere or criticise. Things like this do not usually cause a breakdown, but they can make an already difficult situation worse and provoke the quarrels which ultimately lead to the decision to part.

When this decision is made and the legal steps for separation or divorce put in motion, the problem of the children arises. They are normally placed in the care of the mother unless it is felt that she is unable to undertake this responsibility. But arrangements are usually made for the children to visit the other parent at stated intervals. Sometimes this works out well, but it can be a great strain on the parents, and the children may be baffled by the new relationships. This is particularly the case if the mother marries again and there is a new father in the house.

Some one-parent families consist of a single woman with a child of her own. When the child is born she is faced with a choice: to keep and support the child herself, or to allow it to be adopted by some other family able to provide a more secure and comfortable home. If she has the backing of her own family she may be able to take the child home. If not, she may be able to rent one of the small flatlets that are available for the single woman with a child, or she may find employment where she can take the child with her. But there is likely to be a constant struggle to work full-time and keep her home going on her own. The Finer Report, published in 1974, gives wide coverage to these problems and is useful reading.

The single woman who has never married may have very similar problems to those of the single-parent family, except that she does not have to care for a child as well. But she may have had to spend many years caring for elderly parents or relatives, so that when they die she has few friends or other family contacts to help her. Though the family home will usually be hers, she can suffer great loneliness living there on her own, and find it difficult to fit into any of the social groups in the neighbourhood.

Many of the difficulties in the relationships which have been discussed in this chapter arise through the inability of some people, for one reason or another, to fit into the normal family group. This is especially the case when, as in our contemporary society, the family group is the nuclear one. It should be in the family that children develop and are cared for; it should be to the family that the sick, the elderly, the handicapped and those in trouble can turn. The family should be the resource for those who never marry or whose marriage breaks down. This is normally the case with the extended family. But in our society the State and various voluntary organisations, like the National Council for the Single Woman and her Dependants, often have to come in to help with what the nuclear family is unable to do.

3 Earning and Spending

Having looked at the family and its members in some detail, we now need to see how the family manages to live from day to day and from year to year. This means discovering the different ways in which it obtains the things it needs, or the money that it has to spend – in other words how family members earn their wages or salaries. It also involves looking at how they choose to spend their earnings in view of all the many things they could buy. The question is not just having money available, but spending it in the best possible way, especially where family health and nutrition are concerned. Consumers also need to be sure that what they buy is up to standard; hence the need for some forms of consumer protection.

The National Economy
Before considering the ordinary person, we should see how the country as a whole conducts these affairs. For the country, like its citizens, has to have goods and services and the money to pay for them. If the country can produce plenty of goods and services at a reasonable cost to itself, its citizens will thrive, but if it does not manage to do this, the country is in for hard times.

Goods are what people buy, like food, clothes and motor cars. Services are the things that are done for people and for which they have to pay, such as the provision of trains and buses, waitress-service in restaurants and hairdressing. Most goods are produced by people within the country, though some, like motor cars, may come from abroad.

The total value of the goods and services produced by the workers in this country is called the Gross National Product (GNP). It might be expected that this is what the country has available for its citizens, in other words what it has to spend. But the production of anything takes its toll of the machinery and other equipment used and so the first call on the resources of the country is to make good the depreciation that has taken place as a result of these production processes. So what a country actually has to spend is the GNP less depreciation costs, and this is known as the Net National Product (NNP). To the NNP is added any income from the sale of exports abroad, after the cost of imports has been deducted. So what the country actually has available for its citizens is the NNP plus or minus the difference between revenue from exports and costs of imports.

Earning and Spending 41

But the whole of this NNP does not find its way into the pockets of the people, for the government demands some of it in the form of taxation. What is left after this, is what the people have to spend, and this is called their personal disposable income. Figure 1 should help to make this clear.

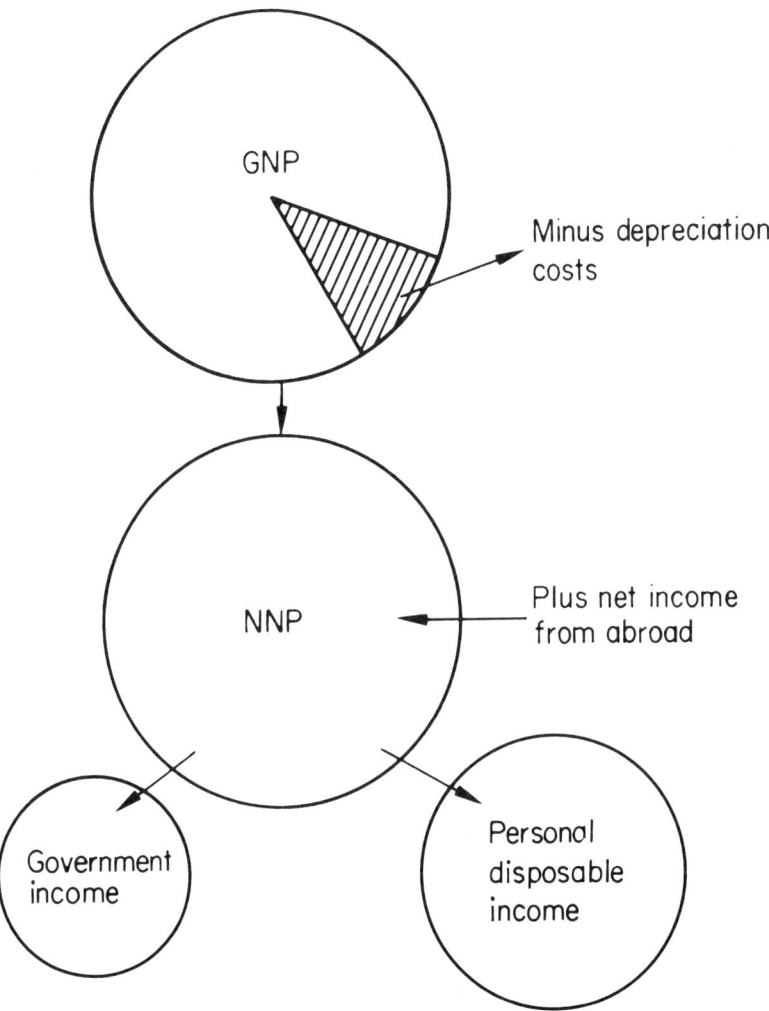

Figure 1 The national economy

42 Home, Family and Community

These days the NNP is almost equally divided between government spending and private spending by individuals. Since the government takes well over 40 per cent of the NNP, it can be said that we have an expanding government sector in this country. The ways in which the government spends the income it gets from its share of the NNP depends on the priorities which it gives to the needs of the moment.

Almost half the government expenditure today goes on social services of one type or another. These include: social security benefits, such as sickness and supplementary benefit; health and personal social services like hospitals, doctors and dentists, cheap milk and welfare foods for the young; educational services such as the building and running of schools, colleges and universities; housing the lower income groups; and providing a clean and wholesome environment for people in general. Quite a large chunk of government expenditure goes on defence, and the rest on a miscellany of things, such as subsidies to industry, trade and transport, the provision of libraries and museums, and the maintenance of law and order by the courts and the police force. All this can be seen in Figure 2.

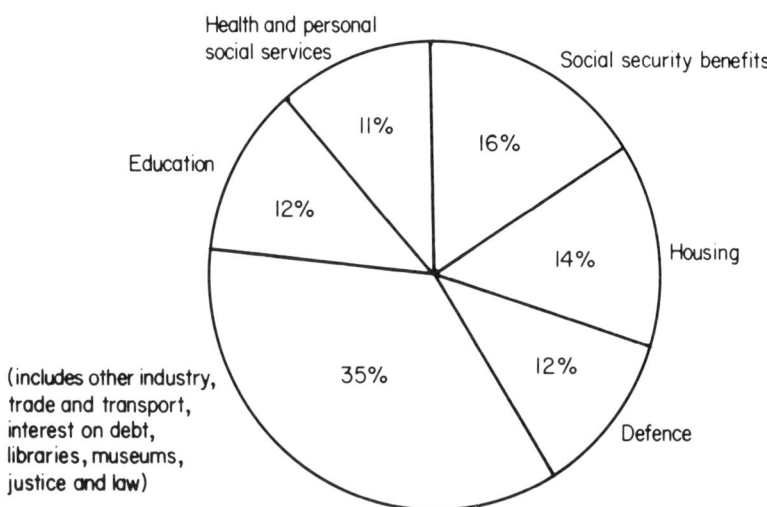

Figure 2   Government expenditure (1975)

What a person has to spend is his disposable income. This is the gross income which he is paid for the work he does (plus any income he receives from other sources such as investments) *minus* the amount the government takes from him in direct taxation. Since most direct taxes are deducted at source, the personal disposable income for most people is what they receive in their pay packet – their 'take-home' pay. This represents the amount available to the individual to spend as he pleases.

Our system of taxation consists of direct and indirect taxes. Direct taxes are levied directly on people, like income tax, and have to be paid by them. Indirect taxes are levied on goods and services, and are paid by the individual either as part of the price of goods, or (and sometimes additionally) by way of Value Added Tax. VAT is indirect because it is a tax on consumption: if the individual does not consume (or buy) he does not pay the tax.

The chief tax which the ordinary person meets in his everyday life is income tax. Income tax is deducted at source from an employee's pay packet by his employer according to a prescribed schedule, and this method is known as PAYE or Pay As You Earn. Each person has a code, which is determined by the size of his taxable income and the allowances to which he is entitled. Periodically he is informed of his code number by his Inspector of Taxes and this code is then implemented by his employer.

Allowances which can be claimed at the moment (1978) include a personal allowance which applies to everyone, children's allowances, an age allowance for elderly people and a wife's earned income relief. Any income remaining after the allowances have been deducted is taxed at the basic rate, which is now 34 per cent (1977–8). Should the income remaining exceed £5,000 an excess tax is charged at higher rates which commence at 40 per cent and eventually reach 83 per cent.

Most teenagers, when they go to work, earn enough to qualify for income tax. This means that they earn more than the basic personal allowance which is free from tax. They may be able to claim additional allowances for a marriage partner or dependants and may get some relief on things like a life assurance premium.

Income from investments is also subject to tax, although there are certain exceptions such as saving certificates which are tax-free. Should income from investments exceed £1,000, further tax – the investment income surcharge – is also payable.

Income from property, usually consisting of rents from property which a person owns and lets, is also subject to tax. There are additional taxes on capital gains, which usually result from the sale of stocks and shares, property or other investments. In the past estate duty had to be paid on property worth more than a certain amount when a person died. Now a capital transfer tax has been introduced. This tax is paid not only on the value of a deceased person's estate, but also on certain gifts made during the person's lifetime.

Our system of taxation is progressive, which means that people with higher incomes have to pay an increasing proportion of their income in tax. A wealth tax is also under consideration, which would probably be charged annually on the value of a person's total wealth, if this is above a certain amount. The result of this progressive tax system is that large sums of money are taken from the more affluent and transferred to the State. Some of this is paid out again, in the form of social benefits and other cheap or free State services, to needier persons. The result is a greater equality in spending power and perhaps fewer people in the lowest and the highest income ranges after taxation has been met.

Earning an Income
Most people have to earn in order to support themselves and their family. Only a very few have enough wealth of their own to be able to live without doing some form of work. Those of us who work follow some form of occupation which will pay us a weekly wage or a monthly salary. Young people start work at the age of sixteen unless they continue their education or training. The age at which they can receive their State retirement pension is sixty-five for men and sixty for women. But some people retire before this age if they have other means of support such as an occupational pension from the firm for which they work, while others prefer to work beyond their pensionable age.

The proportions of men and women in paid employment are about equal in the younger age groups. Most women marry in their twenties and have children, and so the proportion of working women in this age group drops. It begins to rise again in the 30–40 age group and is at its highest in the 40–50 age group. After this age the financial incentive for women to work drops since the children have left home and expenses are less. Many prefer part-time jobs and some enjoy staying at home altogether.

In the past there was a fairly even spread of people over the different occupations, although semi-skilled and unskilled manual work tended to attract the greatest proportion of workers because much of the heavy work in the construction industries was performed by human labour. With the mechanisation of most of the simpler processes, the need for such labour no longer exists, and more people are now engaged in professional, technical and clerical occupations. Nevertheless about one-quarter of all working men and women are employed in some form of manufacturing occupation.

With the rise in the standard of living which has taken place since the Second World War, there has been a great growth in the building industry and in other industries connected with the furnishing and equipment of the home. But the skilled craftsman is disappearing, since the builder now uses brick and prefabricated concrete and furniture and equipment is produced in the factory rather than by the cabinetmaker. Hence there is an increase in the production of prefabricated houses and built-in furniture where the design is of great importance, but individual craftsmanship is almost non-existent.

The developments in science and technology and the use of the computer have led to an increase in the number of people engaged in professions connected with them. Skilled executives are required to direct and manage the work and there is a need for an ever-increasing number of laboratory assistants and technicians. But the unskilled work is now performed by the machines and only a few people are required to watch and control them.

Similarly, with the growth of State control in industry and the development of the welfare services, there has been a rapid increase in the number of people employed by the State as civil servants. A large and increasing proportion of the population is employed in this way, which places a heavy burden on the Exchequer.

The distribution of women in the different occupations is also changing. Previously there was a concentration of women in relatively few occupations like teaching, nursing, clerical and social work. For some time now they have been entering the male-dominated occupations, and since the Sex Discrimination Act, 1975, they are free to compete with men in applying for any sort of job. On the other hand, men are beginning to take some of the top jobs in women's occupations. In the recent formation of the social services departments of the local authorities most of the directors were men, while male nurses are beginning to come to the fore in the nursing profession.

Earnings in these different occupations vary considerably. For the highly skilled and professional person a reasonably high salary is paid. This is because such a person requires a long period of training and experience before he is fully competent. Relatively few people undertake this training, and so the supply of fully trained and equipped people, like accountants and doctors, is small in relation to the demand. This relationship of demand to supply of labour in the different occupations is what originally brought about wage differentials and the evolution of normal or customary rates of wages: for example, what the dustman is paid as compared with the lawyer.

These normal or customary rates for different occupations are being questioned in modern society. Many people feel that the wage should be related more closely to the nature of the work, so that work that is disagreeable, like that of the miner, or involves unsocial hours, should be paid more. This is beginning to happen now that wage rates are reviewed from time to time to try to ensure that they keep pace with rising prices.

Another reason for the change in differentials is because, as prices rise, employers are faced with alternatives. They can make economies by cutting down their work force. But this causes unemployment and so, in spite of redundancy payments, it is not a popular way of meeting the situation. Instead, some pay higher wages to their workers, although this may mean that they have to raise the price of their products. The result is that wages in such an occupation rise more than in others and differentials are altered.

The extent to which employers are forced into this situation depends very much upon the power of the trade unions. Trade union power is unevenly distributed between occupations, and even within occupations themselves, so that where trade union power is strong, wages are likely to rise more quickly and to a greater extent than where it is weak. Also, in industries where a small group of workers hold key positions in the system of production, as they do in the motor trade, the employer may feel that it is better to give them higher wages than to close down the plant. Their wages are then forced out of line with those in other industries and differentials are affected.

The effect on the family of this inflationary situation, which involves a fairly regular and continuous rise in the level of prices, depends on the flexibility with which wages can be adjusted to the price levels of commodities in constant demand, like bread, meat and vegetables. In industry, trade and commerce, wages are likely to respond fairly quickly but in the professions, such as law and medicine, salaries are tied by custom or long-standing agreements, so that there is far less flexibility. The level of the income of the professional classes is not keeping pace with that of other working people. The people who are worst hit by inflation are those with fixed incomes. Many are elderly people living on occupational pensions or on their savings. Their pensions may eventually be adjusted, although there is always a time lag in this. But their savings quickly lose their value.

Consumer Spending

Most households depend on the earnings of those who go out to work. What matters is not so much the amount of money earned and put into the family 'kitty', but what this money will buy. When prices were relatively steady, the family knew more or less what it could afford. It followed a pattern of spending which was typical of its size of income and social class. With inflation, this has become much more blurred, and each family has to be much more selective in its spending.

Some idea of the ways in which families allocate their expenditure can be gained from the *Family Expenditure Survey,* published annually by the Department of Employment and Productivity since 1957. It covers private households of all types, and some 10,000 are contacted throughout the country. Expenditure is classified under the headings: food, housing, fuel, light and power; clothing, footwear and durable goods; other goods and services. Figure 3 gives some idea of how expenditure was distributed over these categories in 1976.

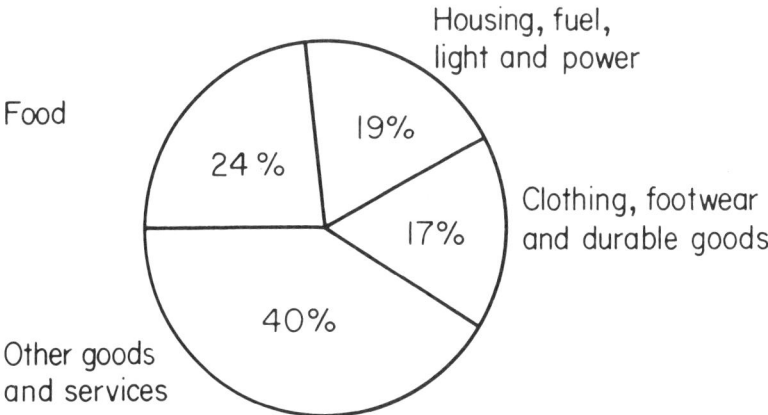

Figure 3 Expenditure for a household with an average income (1976)

It can be seen from Figure 3 that about one-quarter of the family income is spent on food and one-fifth on other things connected with the home, such as housing, fuel, light and power. About one-sixth goes on clothing, footwear and durable household goods, such as furniture and floor coverings, television, electrical and other equipment. 'Other goods' include such things as books, cameras, cosmetics, medicines, toys and pets. Services include anything of a personal nature that is done for the benefit of people in the family, such as meals in restaurants, repairs to the car or hairdressing.

The two most important things which affect family expenditure are the income of the household and the size of the family. Figure 3 relates to a household with an average income. But if the household income was derived almost entirely from social security and supplementary benefits the pattern of expenditure would be somewhat different. Food would take up at least one-third of the total spending; housing, fuel, light and power would be responsible for much of the rest, leaving very little for any clothing or other household goods and services. Old age pensioners, who often come within this category, can afford little beyond their food, rent and heating and even these things can sometimes prove difficult so that the local authority may have to help with rent, and the gas or electricity company permit payments spread throughout the year.

The household with an income well above the average would spend a slightly smaller proportion on food – one-fifth rather than one-quarter. But quite a large proportion of expenditure would be taken up in direct taxes, mortgages, life assurance and various forms of investments. Similarly certain categories of expenditure, like clothes, entertainment, holidays and household equipment, would be relatively greater.

The size of the family can also alter the distribution of expenditure. A large household of some six or seven members would be expected to spend a greater proportion of family income on food, although this increase would not necessarily be in proportion to the number of family members, since cooking on a large scale is more economical than on a small one. The same applies to housing, for although a larger house would be required, family members could economise on living space. Less might be spent on clothes and household goods, although this is not necessarily the case.

The age of family members can make a difference to expenditure. A family with teenage children will spend more on food than one where the members are adults or where the children are younger. Teenagers will want more money for clothes and their own private expenditure, although in many cases they earn this for themselves by newspaper rounds, helping in shops or lending a hand with catering firms at weekends, etc.

The professional family is likely to have a slightly different scale of priorities in expenditure from that of the factory worker. Things like private education for their children and medical expenses may form part of their expenditure. They may live in their own house and so spend more on house maintenance. They may buy fewer convenience foods and so spend less on this. But in the case of occupational spending it is very difficult to generalise.

An item of expenditure which can be very variable is housing, since those who live in London and the south-east have to spend much more on this than those who live further north. In fact, an average family in London can spend as much as 50 per cent more on housing than one which lives in a more remote part of Britain. Similarly the family which lives in a town will usually spend more on housing than one which lives in the country. Though this is often balanced by the fact that the country dweller often has to own a car if he needs a reliable form of transport, while the town dweller may be able to manage without one.

A breakdown of expenditure on different types of food is contained in the *National Food Survey*, published annually since 1940. Selected households are asked to keep a record of all the food they purchase in a week. They are given a log book in which to do this, and are asked to enter the quantity and cost of all the food they buy. They are also asked to state the number and age of the members of the household, any meals which a member of the family takes outside the home, in a factory canteen, at school or in any other way. Provided the housewife is not buying in to add to her stocks, this should provide a good indication of the quality and cost of food that is consumed by the average household.

Looking back to the end of rationing in the mid-fifties, three somewhat different consumption patterns can be seen. During the war and post-war rationing period, families consumed very much the same because they could not easily buy anything different. But in the fifties their diet gradually reverted to the more traditional patterns linked with income, type of occupation and family composition, although there were no longer the large pre-war disparities between the different income groups. In the sixties convenience foods began to come onto the market and found a place in the diet of those who could afford them, especially in families where the wife went out to work and had little time to devote to the preparation and cooking of food. The higher wage levels of the seventies brought larger incomes to many families. A proportion of this was spent on food, though much went on a family car and a certain amount on alcoholic drinks, particularly wine, which many learnt to drink for the first time on holiday on the Continent.

Very generally, a look at food surveys during the seventies shows that the average consumption of cheese, pork, poultry, convenience meat foods, fruit, instant coffee and quick-frozen foods is rising, while that of liquid milk, beef, lamb, eggs, fish, margarine, sugar preserves, potatoes, bread and flour-produced products is declining. Cream, butter and bacon are fairly constant. So the carbohydrate content of the diet is becoming slightly less, which is as might be expected when heavy manual work is undertaken less frequently, and more money is available for spending on food.

Income plays an important part in determining expenditure on different types of food. Households in the higher income groups will spend more on fresh fruit and other low energy foods and less on high energy foods like bread and potatoes. They consume more dairy produce, carcass meat, bacon, poultry, quick frozen vegetables, breakfast cereals, coffee and proprietary drinks like Ovaltine. In the lower income groups vegetable fats, sugar, white bread, cake and biscuits are more predominant. This is particularly the case with pensioners, partly because they cannot afford much in the way of convenience foods, but also because of the trouble involved in preparing a cooked meal, and the difficulties of chewing meat, vegetables, and other food which is hard.

Social class can have some effect upon the diet of older people, since the income of the middle classes tends to rise only gradually, reaching a peak in the 50–60 age group, and does not fall nearly as much on retirement as does that of the ordinary worker. This means that middle class people can maintain very much the same pattern of consumption throughout their lives, and the elderly are usually able to afford a variety of suitable foods other than bread and cakes. How long this statement remains true will depend upon the extent of inflation. For the elderly person who depends on investment income is likely to suffer most from a fall in the value of money.

Geographical location has its effects upon the consumption of food. Towns come off better than country districts because food tends to be transported to them in bulk. Thus London has a much larger consumption of fresh fruit and vegetables and meat than many other parts of the country. People living in country districts are often unable to buy the products that are grown in their own area. Thus the north has a low consumption of milk, while Scotland is lacking in fresh vegetables and fruit. People living in a rural area often have to go to the nearest town to buy their fresh fruit and vegetables if they do not grow them themselves.

An increasing amount of money now goes on buying and maintaining various forms of equipment for the home. Almost every family has a television set and usually colour, which is expensive to hire or buy, and for which the licence is costly, although it may now be paid in instalments. Most families have a vacuum cleaner, a washing machine and a refrigerator. A deep freeze is almost essential in a family where the mother is in a full-time job. Though more expensive to use, it is easy and quick and many meals can be prepared in advance and placed in the freezer. A tumble drier is a favoured purchase, particularly by those who live in flats or maisonettes where there are few outdoor or indoor drying facilities. A dishwasher and a rotary ironer fall rather low on the list and are often owned by those in some special circumstance, a dishwasher by the large family or one in which people have most or all of their meals at home, and an ironer where there is a great deal of laundry or the housewife needs to sit to do her ironing.

Income seems to play little part in the ownership of these appliances, for some of the poorest families possess several, and the more well-to-do family may be without many of them. They can be very much a status symbol. If one person buys one, other people in the road will often do so. On the other hand, an appliance is frequently purchased to meet some special need. This may happen with a deep freeze when a family has a large fruit or vegetable garden. It may be easier and cheaper to freeze the surplus than to use the older methods of bottling and preserving.

Not only have people in recent decades had more money to spend on a variety of products, but the fact that many are now made in nylon and plastic attracts custom. They are often cheaper than when made in natural materials, and at the same time may last longer. There is now scarcely any kind of clothing or furnishing fabric which cannot be bought in nylon, and plastic is used widely for household equipment, such as food containers, cooking utensils, etc.

The age group which has greatly increased its demand for products are teenagers. Young people today provide a market of their own. At school leaving age a young person can earn a reasonably good wage and has few commitments except to hand over a small sum to parents for board and lodging. The rest can be spent on clothes, cosmetics, entertainment, drink and cigarettes or anything else the young person fancies. He or she will demand particular goods and services and many commercial enterprises now cater for their needs. Dance halls, discotheques, coffee bars, restaurants and other places of amusement, with their own special furnishings and lighting, are provided for young people. They can buy their clothes from boutiques in places like Carnaby Street which supply their own particular styles, and their hi-fi and cassettes from shops which cater especially for them. Trade flourishes because the demand for these goods and services is reasonably large and constant.

Retail Marketing
Shops in the towns used to be concentrated almost entirely in or around the High Street. Residential areas had their own small corner shop, and in the rural areas there was the village store. Important changes have been taking place in the pattern of retailing, as can be seen from the *Report of the Census of Distribution and other Services, 1961*. The number of shops has fallen by some 60,000 in the last ten years or so, and the average size of shops is increasing. This is especially true of the food stores which expect the purchaser to make only an occasional visit and then to do most of her shopping there. Small traders are finding that High Street rents are rising beyond their reach, and so are having to move to the side streets.

This does not mean that the small trader is being forced out of existence. The number of such shops is still quite large, especially in the suburbs and country districts. The main things that keep them going are their attentive personal service with the possibility of delivery of goods, their long and unsocial hours (some stay open for a time on Sundays and bank holidays), their readiness to accept only a small profit on their capital investment, and the fact that they are accessible to those, particularly the elderly, who are unable to travel to the main shopping centres. By joining voluntary wholesale buying groups like Mace, and by providing a certain amount of self-service, they are able to keep their customers and cut their costs.

Shopping can be highly competitive. We see this when we go from shop to shop to find the best bargains. So the problem of cutting costs is important for the shopkeeper. There are certain costs which the smaller shops have to bear which could be spread more widely if they were bigger. This is the principle on which the multiple retailer works. He owns shops in a number of neighbouring towns or throughout the country as a whole, which sell similar types of goods but are under individual management. Such shops can take advantage of bulk trading and can make good bargains with manufacturers because of the size of their orders. They can employ specialists for such purposes as advertising and display, accounting and staff management. But they also keep the advantage of the small local trader. Many of them, like Boots, Marks and Spencer, and Woolworth, are household names.

The predecessor of these multiple shops was the co-operative store, which came into being in the middle of the nineteenth century to meet the needs of working people who were living in the densely populated towns. Such people were more often than not the victims of poverty and unemployment. They were tied to the corner shop because they owed money to the shopkeeper and could therefore be forced to accept poor quality goods.

The aim of the seven flannel-weavers in Rochdale who opened the first co-operative store in 1844 in Toad Lane, was to run a shop themselves in which goods would be sold for cash at cost price to those who were registered with them. Each registered member had to buy a share and received a dividend at the end of the year related to the amount of purchases he had made at the shop. No credit was allowed and all profits made had to be distributed in this way to the members.

The popularity of this form of trading spread rapidly, and co-operative stores were opened throughout the country, particularly in the industrial areas. They managed to keep their costs down through a central buying agency, the Co-operative Wholesale Society, which among other things owned tea plantations in Ceylon, had its own biscuit factory and its own bank. Since goods were by then sold at market price in their shops, the difference between this and costs provided a good dividend (or 'divi', as it was known) for members.

All this was possible because the goods people could afford were largely necessities of life which were very similar in type. By the end of the Second World War the income of working people had risen greatly and they were able to buy many things which were not necessities and so to exercise a far wider choice than the co-operative stores supplied. The consumers' co-operative movement suffered, and in 1958 the Gaitskell Commission was appointed to investigate the situation and recommend changes. The result has been that although the control of the co-operative is still in the hands of its members who are its customers and who have equal voting rights, the dividend in England now takes the form of trading stamps and the Co-op seems very little different from the ordinary multiple shop.

Department stores, which came into the foreground in the late nineteenth century, were the result of the move of the middle class to the suburbs combined with the possibility of a day's shopping trip by suburban railway or the horse omnibus to the centre of the large cities. They were large shops, in a central position like Oxford Street in London, which sold in their different departments a wide variety of goods for use in the home. Harrods is an outstanding example. Started in 1849 as a small grocer's shop to meet the needs of the wealthy living in the Knightsbridge area of London, it gradually expanded its commodities to include clothing, furniture and many other requisites for the home, and now offers practically everything, from a pets' corner to foreign travel and a banking section. Its main attraction is that it sells goods which are slightly different from those found in other shops, in surroundings of spaciousness and opulence not found in other departmental stores. It manages to thrive largely through its tourist clientele.

Most other department stores started in a small way and gradually expanded. Peter Robinson, for instance, had a single shop in Oxford Street, and gradually acquired the shops adjacent to it until it had taken over its present corner site on Oxford Circus. John Lewis was a buyer at Peter Robinson's before he opened his own shop almost next door.

Many other departmental stores, like Marshall and Snelgrove, and Swan and Edgar, have found in recent years that their middle class customers can no longer afford what they used to buy. At the same time the cost of running such shops has risen phenomenally. This has led to a massive takeover by companies like the House of Fraser and Debenhams, so that although some of the stores have kept their original name and character, most of them are, in fact, part of one of these companies.

Another recent change is for the big department stores to open branches in the provinces and the wealthier suburbs where there is still a large middle class demand. The Army and Navy, which was originally a co-operative for families of those serving in the armed forces, has done this. Debenhams is doing much the same thing, though in a different way, by buying out existing department stores in the large cities.

An increasing number of people are shopping at the older multiples such as Marks and Spencer, Woolworth and British Home Stores. This is partly because such shops have paid more attention to quality in recent years and are willing to exchange articles which do not come up to standard or the customer's requirements. Large mass production makes it possible to charge lower prices and this, combined with the present low value of the pound compared with many foreign currencies, prompts shoppers to come over on day-tickets from the Continent and purchase many of their requirements in London and the coastal towns. The multiples have started selling a much greater variety of goods, including food, so that they are hardly distinguishable from the department store.

Perhaps the most noticeable change has been the development of self-service instead of customer-service in shops and catering establishments. The reason for this has been the rapid rise in the wages that have to be paid to staff, and the social security contributions required from the employer, even though staff may only be working part-time. Self-service requires an attractive display of a wide range of inviting goods which can be collected from the shelves by the customer, combined with a streamlined method of paying. This saves labour and the shopkeeper is able to spread the work of his staff more evenly over the day and week, even though the numbers of customers may fluctuate. But it has the disadvantage of encouraging shoplifting. It can be easy for a customer to slip a few articles into his or her bag and fail to pay for them at the check-out.

The name supermarket is given to large self-service shops with at least three check-points. They may be owned by the Co-op or some of the older multiples like Sainsbury, or they may be newer concerns like Tesco, or of American origin like Safeway. They are popular because they offer convenience and speed to the shopper with a comprehensive selection of food and other household articles at competitive prices, and also have high standards of hygiene, packing and refrigeration. The scale on which they operate gives them low costs and an efficient use of labour which enable them to buy expensive sites in the main street, to cut prices and offer bargains. They are particularly attractive to working wives who want to do a week's shopping at a time and they often have a late-night opening. Their car parking facilities attract those who live outside the town and women with young children who do not want to wander from shop to shop.

These facilities are accentuated by the hypermarket which is a very large self-service store built outside the town but with easy access to several suburbs. It has a large car park and is very popular on the Continent and in America. In this country it has not been received so well, partly because local planners have withheld their permission and partly because a much smaller percentage of British housewives do their shopping by car.

Brent Cross shopping centre

Britain's answer to the congested High Street is the modern shopping centre, like the Bull Ring in Birmingham or the shopping centre at Brent Cross in London. Centres like these comprise a large variety of shops on more than one level. They are protected from the weather and are traffic free, have their own car park but are also close to public transport. They offer the convenience of being able to obtain all the goods wanted under a single roof and are sometimes called 'one-stop' shopping centres. But like the old Co-ops, their success depends on the stocking of a limited range of choices in a wide variety of everyday articles. The shopper who wants something out of the ordinary will usually have to go elsewhere. Many of the smaller towns are following this pattern of shopping in a modified way by having traffic free areas in the centre of the town so that the shopper can walk easily and safely from one shop to another.

Other modern forms of shopping, mostly American in origin, include discount houses, cash and carry stores and mail order. Discount houses are able to offer rates lower than the manufacturers' retail prices because they are usually on the outskirts of the town and so do not occupy expensive sites in established shopping areas. They pay very little attention to display and do not provide any after-service. Cash and carry stores also offer substantial price reductions, because goods are bought in large quantities and called for by car. Buying by mail order is rapidly becoming an important form of selling, either by post, or through an agent who calls at the house. The customer is able to make his purchase without going out, to choose from an elaborately illustrated catalogue, to order by measurement in many cases, and to match colours. It is very useful when there are small children who cannot be left, or where the customer is out at work all day.

It would seem that these modern innovations have entirely replaced the older methods of shopping, like the mobile shop and the street market. Yet both of these still exist, the mobile shop often as part of some regular roundsman's delivery service, like that of the milkman, while street markets are still held regularly in many towns.

The rise in personal income and the comparative security that this offers has meant that shops now view credit buying much more favourably. In the past it was largely high-priced goods, like furniture, household appliances and motor cars, that people considered buying on credit. Now many more things are purchased in this way.

This may be done through a hire-purchase agreement which means that the goods are paid for in instalments but do not become the purchaser's property until they have been paid for in full. Until then, they belong to the shopkeeper or the lender of the money, although there are legal safeguards to prevent them being taken back without warning.

Earning and Spending 57

A credit sale differs from hire-purchase in that the goods belong to the shopper at once, though the method of payment is by instalments. This form of credit is very popular with goods on mail order and in every case interest is charged for the temporary loan of the money.

Some shops allow their customers credit in the form of monthly accounts, which have to be met by the end of the month in which they are rendered, after which interest has to be paid. A budget account or revolving credit differs from this in that customers pay an agreed amount each month but are allowed to spend in excess of this in any one month. Thus clothes may be bought up to £50 repaying at £2 per month on a budget account, but if the customer has revolving credit, as he repays, he can repurchase, providing he does not exceed the £50 limit.

A comparatively recent introduction is the credit card which lets a person pay for goods or services, usually up to a fixed amount, just by producing the card. Access and Barclay cards, which are issued by the banks, are examples of this method. If a settlement is made when the statement is presented, no interest is charged, but if not, a fairly high rate of interest is demanded for any arrears in payment.

Since even credit cannot meet the high costs of personal service these days, many do-it-yourself and bulk methods of supply are becoming popular. Launderettes are replacing laundries and many factories are using automatic vending machines in place of canteen services. Motels, which offer motorists overnight accommodation that is largely self-service, are appearing along our highways. Travel agencies reduce their costs by package tours which involve block bookings of hotels and their own special bulk-rate transport. Every effort is being made to save the cost of personal service and at the same time to provide new forms of product to the average customer. Market research helps to decide which of these various products are attractive to the public and trade fairs, like the Ideal Home Exhibition, make them known to wide numbers of people.

Consumer Interests

This great increase in the size and scope of consumption of different goods and services makes it increasingly necessary for consumers to protect themselves. In the past things were more simple and standardised, and consumers could often see at a glance whether goods came up to the standard of what they wanted. Now there are pre-packed goods in great variety which cannot easily be examined; synthetic fibres which need special care in washing, drying and ironing; and various domestic appliances which are complicated mechanisms and can and do go wrong.

The consumer has always found it difficult to demand his rights because usually he is a single individual with little power of his own, up against a well-established manufacturer or shop. Therefore legislation for the protection of the consumer has existed for a very long time. Ensuring a uniform weights and measures system throughout the country was one of the declared objects of Magna Carta in 1215. Its modern counterpart, the Weights and Measures Act, 1963, deals largely with pre-packed goods, especially those on supermarket shelves. It prescribes the quantities in which goods like milk can be sold and it makes it an offence to mark goods with a wrong indication of their amount. One of the difficulties of our entrance into the Common Market is that weights and measures are now being quoted in metric terms, which until they have been in use for some time will mean little to the shopper.

The general law relating to the sale of goods is contained in the Sale of Goods Act, 1893, which has been amended by the Supply of Goods (Implied Terms) Act, 1973. When a person buys something in a shop he enters into a legally binding contract with that shop. Once a shopkeeper has agreed to sell, he takes on obligations to the purchaser, which are defined in these acts. The goods he sells must be of merchantable quality; for example, a washing machine, when plugged in, should function properly. The goods must be fit for the purpose for which they are normally used and they must meet the description applied to them. If any of these conditions are not met, then the retailer has broken the contract and the purchaser has the right to return the goods and ask for his money back.

A special case of this is the Unsolicited Goods and Services Act, 1971. Traders cannot demand payment for goods which people have not ordered, such as Christmas cards or labels sent through the post. All they can do is to ask for them back again within six months. After that the goods can be kept by the person to whom they were sent.

Trade marks and trade descriptions are found on many goods. The Trade Descriptions Act, 1968, makes it necessary for a trader to describe what he is selling accurately. If the hotel at which you have booked is said to be one kilometre from the beach, this must be the case. Similarly sale prices must be genuine and should indicate the original price. This act covers many different kinds of descriptions – where goods are made, who made them, how they work and so on.

The consumer is protected from sales talk, sales literature and advertising by the Misrepresentation Act, 1967. If a person has been induced to enter into a contract for sale by the deliberate withholding of material facts by the seller, or by an inaccurate description which conceals some important facts, then there may be a breach of contract.

Provisions governing the sale of food and drugs are contained in the Food and Drugs Act, 1955. This act makes it an offence to describe food falsely or to mislead people about its nature, substance or quality, including its nutritional value. There are also regulations about the containers in which food can be stored or sold, the length of time that it can be kept, and the cleanliness of the premises. Food containers such as jars and tins must show a list of the ingredients in order of weight. Authorised officers of the local authority are empowered to take samples of food offered for sale for analysis to see that they conform to the required regulations, and much the same applies to the sale of drugs.

Some goods may be unsafe, or cause death or serious injury when used. The Consumer Protection Act, 1961, covers these. The act contains regulations about such things as electrical appliance colour codes, safety of carrycot stands, oil heaters, fireguards, lead content in pencils, the flammability of children's nightdresses, etc.

Advertisements have always played upon the susceptibilities of the consumer. Vance Packard, in his books, particularly *The Hidden Persuaders*, has drawn attention to this. For example, he tries to explain why the housewife buys much more than she intends when she goes to a supermarket; and why children like cereals that are said to crackle and crunch.

Legislation can only control advertisement when it causes a nuisance to the public, as can be the case with some postal displays, loudspeakers and aerial advertising; or when it is incorrect or misleading, and then it comes under the Merchandise Marks Acts and the Food and Drugs Acts. The Independent Television Authority, which is allowed to intersperse its programmes with advertisements, has drawn up a code with the government regulating standards and practices for its advertisements, and where products can be harmful to health, such as cigarettes, the government insists on a health warning forming part of the advertisement.

The Molony Committee, set up in 1959 to review the success of existing legislation, recommended that the consumer should be more fully represented. The result was the formation in 1963 of the first consumer group – the Consumer Council. This council was intended to keep itself informed about consumer problems and to provide consumers with advice and guidance. But, though structured and financed by the government, it had no statutory powers. Any complaints had to be taken to the local Citizens' Advice Bureau which would take action with the appropriate government department.

The Council was wound up in 1970 and instead, the Fair Trading Act, 1973, provided for a Director-General of Fair Trading with wide new powers and his own staff to inquire into any trade practices affecting consumers. He does not consider individual complaints. They still have to be dealt with locally. But he publishes all

60 Home, Family and Community

kinds of information so that people know what their rights are and where they can go for help. He encourages trade organisations to institute voluntary codes of practice which all their members accept. He proposes new laws to plug loopholes in existing ones; and he tracks down traders who persistently commit offences. The government department to which he is responsible is the Department of Prices and Consumer Protection, which keeps a general watch on industry and commerce and the protection of the ordinary citizen.

An important aspect of consumer protection is the maintenance of standards. The British Standards Institution (BSI), which originated at the beginning of the century to control standards in industry, now protects consumers through the use of certification marks. Their 'kitemark' appears on goods which have reached its specifications. Other organisations follow a similar practice. The Design Council, which is

Consumer protection marks

partly financed by the government and has its Centre in the Haymarket in London, has its label for products which are well designed, pleasant to look at and practical in use. Care labels are used by some organisations, like the Home Laundering Consultative Council, to indicate exactly how a garment should be washed or cleaned.

In some cases consumers have formed their own group to further their interests. This was the case with the Consumers' Association, which was started in 1957 to 'raise and maintain the standard of goods and services'. It does this mainly by publishing in its monthly magazine *Which?* the results of independent comparative tests on named brands of consumer goods and services. Several types of goods are dealt with each month and a recommendation is usually made as to which of the different types examined is thought to be the best buy. *Which?* is sold entirely through subscriptions and cannot be bought on a bookstall, although it finds its way into the reading room of most factories, offices and other organisations.

The success of the Consumers' Association has encouraged the starting of independent groups, covering a town or region, which unlike the Consumers' Association do take up clients' complaints with retailers and manufacturers. These consumers' aid centres vary in their work according to the type of district they serve and the needs of the clients in the area. But they always give pre-shopping advice and monitor prices in the local shops. They frequently share premises with the Citizens' Advice Bureau and they quite often organise displays on such matters as dealing with accidents in the home, and safety devices.

The larger local authorities are now beginning to take over the responsibility of advising shoppers themselves through their consumer protection departments (which used to be called 'Weights and Measures'). They are opening Consumer Advice Centres where advice and help are given on consumer problems, so that shoppers have enough information on which to base their choice and save themselves unnecessary expense.

However efficient the consumer organisations and the government may be, bad quality and standards will prevail unless the public are taught to recognise them. Therefore consumer education is now taking its place as one of the most important aspects of consumer protection. A wide range of explanatory leaflets and booklets is available at most consumer advice centres and at the Citizens' Advice Bureaux, and staff are trained to answer questions and suggest consumer subjects which could be discussed in groups. Lectures are arranged for schools on all aspects of consumer protection and consumer studies occupy a part of the curriculum of most comprehensive and secondary schools for the 15+ age group.

It is not only the individual consumer who needs educating. Consumers as a whole should have a unified policy. For consumers demand a great deal of what is produced by the nation, and if they stand out for good quality and high standards, manufacturers will be more likely to produce goods of this nature. Not only will individual shoppers be more satisfied with what they can buy, but the nation as a whole will gain a reputation for good quality and high standards which should increase our exports and so add to the wealth of the community.

4 Work and Leisure

Human beings have always had to work in order to live. Work is an essential feature of life. Yet a person does not work all the time. He has periods of work and periods of leisure. In pre-industrial societies this distinction between work and leisure was not always clearly marked. A man was at work from dawn to dusk, although if the weather was poor or there was little to do, he was not necessarily actively working all the time. He might stop to talk and then resume again. In a modern industrial society those who work do so for agreed periods and when they are not working their time is their own.

Yet even today, when it is possible to indicate the number of hours that are actually spent at work, it is not so easy to say exactly how much time is real leisure. This is because there are certain fringe activities which are neither work nor leisure, like a husband helping in the house or putting the children to bed, or a single woman doing her own housework and laundry at the weekend. Things like these have to be done whether the person wants to or not, but they are not part of his or her work schedule, nor are they leisure activities. It is only when these demands, as well as those of work, have been met, that a person can be said to be free to do what he likes with the rest of his time. Housework in any case can be a full-time (unpaid) job. Thus leisure may be described in the words of a recent government social survey, *Planning for Leisure:* 'The period when a person is not in paid employment or travelling to and from such employment or, in the case of a housewife or mother, when not engaged in domestic duties or caring for the essential needs of the family.'

Work in Relation to Leisure
Nineteenth century industrialisation in Britain brought about big changes in the relation of work to leisure. In pre-industrial society it was the job rather than the hours that counted. In both the fields and the workshop a man was fairly free to choose when he worked, provided he kept up with the job he had been given. But when he went to work in a factory his hours were governed by the times that the factory was open and by the fact that he was only doing one small process in the manufacture of some product, and so he had to fit in with the other workers if the final product was to be produced on time. This could often involve very long hours and hardly any leisure at all.

One of the purposes of trade unions, which were formed in the second half of the nineteenth century, was to regulate hours of work. They were reasonably successful and gradually hours were reduced until today the average worker is employed for about forty-four hours per week. This does not always indicate the time that is actually worked for many people prefer to work more than these hours in order to increase their pay. Since overtime is paid at a higher rate than normal hours of work, many workers are willing to do it. In fact, in some industries, the workers reckon that they should always do a certain amount of overtime and are ready to strike if this opportunity is not given to them.

In some industries a shift system is worked, which means that there are usually three shifts of eight hours in a day. Such industries are usually those using expensive capital equipment which has to be kept running continuously if it is to pay its way. Personal service occupations, like hospitals, where continuous care is needed, are another example. In many cases, shift workers are paid more than other workers, especially if they have to work 'unsocial' hours on a shift, outside the normal working day. This frequently appeals to the married man who has a large family to support and needs the extra money. Sometimes husband and wife like to work shifts so that one or other of them is at home to look after the children. Quite often a nurse is willing to work a late shift in order to fit in with her husband for whom a late shift may be the normal working day.

In the nineteenth century workers had to work a good deal harder than they do today. They therefore had very little leisure and did not have the problem of what to do with it. They were mostly too tired to do anything other than rest. Management, on the other hand, were able to take expensive holidays abroad and amuse themselves in many other ways. The position is now somewhat reversed. It is the working people who have their weekends and evenings free and are faced with the problem of what to do with their leisure time. The executive is frequently very tied up with his work, and even in his free time is often engaged in doing something related to it, such as attending conferences or bringing his knowledge of the job up to date.

The amount of leisure which women have depends on their occupation. If a woman is a housewife her leisure is governed by her home ties. Sometimes home ties, like a sick husband, young children, or an elderly or handicapped relative, may occupy the greater part of her time and give her very little leisure indeed. Then, although she is not paid, she is working as hard as any person in employment. On the other hand, if she has no children, or if they have left home, she has plenty of leisure time in which to do what she wants.

Before the First World War women of the middle class very rarely worked for pay. Their menfolk were expected to keep them, and as they had plenty of servants, they were relieved of most household chores. In fact it was almost impossible for a middle class married woman to do paid work, for she was surrounded by so many restrictions. When Queen Victoria came to the throne in 1837, the middle class wife and all her possessions belonged to her husband, and if she left him he could force her to return to him or refuse to support her; and since she had no rights of her own regarding her children, he could refuse her access to them. Any money she had on marriage or any she acquired after her marriage belonged to her husband and she had no rights regarding the family income.

The first important landmark in the process of emancipation was the Matrimonial Causes Act, 1857, which allowed the wife the separate use of any property acquired by her during a judicial separation. Then, in 1870, women were allowed to keep anything they earned up to £200, and in 1882 a man no longer had any right to his wife's property on marriage. Various changes have taken place since then, but the married woman is still not taxed in the same way as a single woman. Although she can decide to be taxed on her earned income separately from her husband, this is only advantageous when the husband's income and the wife's earnings are both high.

A further reason for the difficulty that the middle class woman experienced in finding employment was her lack of education for a world dominated by men. She was taught at home by a governess, and it was only when it became possible for boys and girls to receive a similar secondary education that it became feasible for middle class women to find employment.

Even then it was some time before occupations were opened to them. In spite of her qualifications, it took Elizabeth Garrett Anderson some ten years to be accepted as a woman doctor, and even then she had difficulty in getting patients who were in a position to pay. Except for nursing, teaching and social work, which were regarded as women's occupations, it has taken a long time to break down the prejudice against the employment of women in the professions. For instance, in spite of the Sex Discrimination Act, 1975, which amongst other things is intended to ensure that men and women have equal opportunities for finding employment, they are still not recognised for ordination in the Established Church.

Women in the lower income groups have not had to face this discrimination, for poverty made it necessary for them to work in order to support themselves and their families. Before the Industrial Revolution most of them were employed in domestic service, in the workshops or in the fields, and their relative contribution to the national product was large, probably even greater than it is today. The same thing is true at the moment of the developing countries, where women supply a great part of rural labour. With the coming of industrialisation to this country in the late eighteenth and early nineteenth centuries, poverty forced women of the working class to work either in the factories, or in the homes of the middle class as domestic servants. Many married women were employed as washer-women and seamstresses because they could do such work in their own homes. But they were paid a pittance for it, and their health suffered because they had to work such long hours to earn so little.

The only instance of married women being employed for their worth was in the Lancashire cotton industry where their skilled work was greatly valued because they had more dexterity than men. For many years they were the only group of married women who expected to continue in employment when they had families of their own, and who were not forced to do this through sheer poverty.

Wartime drew many other married women into work. During the First World War they were taken on as skilled workers in a wide variety of industries to replace men who had gone to fight. In the Second World War, if their children were of school age, they were mobilised for work in munition and other factories connected with war time needs. With the increasing labour shortage, part-time shifts and other concessions were introduced for them so that women with domestic responsibilities could do their share.

The part that women played in the war effort gave them the chance to be treated more fairly in comparison with men. This was seen in the political field when, after the 1914-18 war, women over the age of thirty were allowed to vote, although it was not until 1928 that all women of twenty-one and over were given the right to vote. Since the age of majority is now eighteen, everyone of this age and over can vote if they wish to do so.

In the economic field women did manage to hold their own and to make slow but steady progress. The gay twenties was a decade in which women entered into an increasing number of different occupations. They were no longer confined to traditional women's work like domestic service, light factory work, teaching, nursing and social work. They began to take up various forms of secretarial work in large numbers, almost replacing men in this area. Many more women were employed in catering trades and in the professions. Women's skills began to be recognised in occupations which affected the home, and such organisations as the Electrical Association for Women (1924), the Women's Gas Federation (1935) and the Women's Advisory Council on Solid Fuel (1943), came into being. The Council of Scientific Management in the Home (1932), which is now a specialist committee of the Women's Group on Public Welfare, came into being to study and advise on the design and equipment of the home. They had the advantage of looking at the subject from the point of view of the person who did the housework.

The wars also demonstrated that the work of married women was acceptable and needed. At the beginning of this century, only 25 per cent of all employable women were out at work and the majority of these were under the age of thirty-five and unmarried. Most women left paid employment when they married and did not return to it again. This was the origin of the idea that women were most useful in semi-skilled and repetitive work. It was not worth the expense and trouble of training them for anything else if they were going to leave for good on marriage.

Further possibilities for the employment of women opened up with the new light industries that appeared in this century to help maintain and enhance the standard of living of most people. They are closely related to furnishing and equipping the home, the provision of radio and television parts, and the many mechanical operations needed by the new technology. Such industries are not hampered by the tradition that men should be employed to do the work, and they are far more flexible with regard to part-time and intermittent work which many married women require when their families are young.

Since the Second World War a further change has been taking place, the return to work of married women when their children are off their hands. This has come about because of the earlier marriages and the fact that most mothers have had their last child by the time they have reached thirty. At that age, the average woman still has almost half a century ahead of her. Even if she waits until the youngest child is an adolescent before working, she is unlikely to be more than forty-five, with at least fifteen years of working life before her.

Thus the female working population is now mostly married, and a good proportion of them are in their middle years. This means that they have families to care for, homes to run and a constant pull between the demands of their employment and those of their home. These have to be reconciled if they are to live happy and contented lives.

Working Wives

In come countries, like the Soviet Union, the employment of married women does not present a problem. Unless they have very young children, married women are expected to work and facilities like nursery schools and late shopping hours are available to make it possible for them to do so. The main reason for this situation has been the great demand for workers needed to turn a country which was predominantly agricultural into a highly industrialised state, and to do so in the shortest space of time.

In Britain, however, there has not been such a need and so fairly well-defined traditional ideas have grown up on what constitutes the tasks of a wife and mother. A woman is expected to make it her first duty to run the home efficiently and care for the children adequately. Since domestic help is now not easily available this can be a time-consuming and monotonous job. At the same time she is expected to be an attractive companion to her husband when he is at home, to be available to go out with him and to entertain friends. This means that she must not be completely submerged in domesticity or out at work when needed.

The responsibility for the care and upbringing of the children generally lies with the mother. The result is that she looks after them when they are young and when they are ill, and so they come to her when things go wrong. It is usually the mother who is consulted when the children have families of their own, and who is called in to help with an emergency.

Some women are quite content with a life of domesticity, but others prefer to have a job outside the home. There are various reasons for this. The most usual one is because they need the money to keep up the standard of living which they have set for themselves and their family. This applies particularly to women in the lower income groups where a little extra money when the children are growing up makes all the difference to the activities and comfort of the family.

Where a woman is unhappy in her relationship with her husband or finds one of the children very difficult, she may obtain some solace and relief in work outside the home. Similarly in cases of incipient mental disturbance a job is often suggested as a means of reducing tension and helping a woman to adjust to her circumstances.

A job may be sought to relieve the monotony of housework or to escape from loneliness. The smaller size of the family today and modern domestic equipment make it possible for a woman to be at home most of the day and yet have little to do and a large amount of spare time to fill. Modern housing cuts families off from their neighbours, especially if they live in blocks of flats or have recently moved to a new housing estate, and the housewife can feel very isolated.

There are also a number of women who have given up a career which they very much enjoyed for marriage. Many of them have undergone a long training for this career and their job seems an essential part of their life. They want to return to work as soon as possible, not for the money that the job offers, but because they enjoy it.

The conflict between their home responsibilities and the attractions of a job can give rise to much tension in some women. This is caused not so much by the practical difficulties of organising the home so that the various tasks can be done, as by the fear that relationships within the home, with husband and children, may be affected. Modern psychologists, like John Bowlby, insist that the first five years of a child's life are all-important to his future if he is to grow up into a normal, healthy and self-reliant person. During this time, they say, the child needs the love and care of his parents, particularly his mother, in order that he may develop in an atmosphere of safety and security. If she goes out to work, the child may be permanently harmed.

On the other hand there is the view that, provided suitable arrangements are made for the care of the child, this is not likely. Children in the past were brought up by nannies without any obvious harm to most of them. If the child is left in the care of a grandmother, another relative or a friend, or even in a day nursery, while the mother is at work, it is unlikely that his development will be impaired.

With older children, it is said that the mother's absence from home can lead to delinquency. The picture is that of the latch-key child who wears the front-door key on a chain round his neck, so that he can let himself in on his return from school, get his own supper and put himself to bed. Boredom leads him to gang up with similar children and they terrorise the neighbourhood. Again, there is no conclusive evidence for this, nor that such a child will get himself into trouble with the law. Some do and publicity is given to the fact, but many do not.

Viola Klein, in her book *Britain's Married Women Workers*, goes into the effects of maternal employment on children in some detail. Her view is that there is very little direct influence on the lives and development of the children. Only when there is a deficiency of maternal love, poor discipline at home and lack of family cohesion, are any bad effects produced. It is therefore the personality of the mother, the nature of the substitute care and the provision of adequate arrangements in case of emergency that really matter.

One of Viola Klein's unexpected findings was that mothers who worked showed a better adjustment to their children than those who stayed at home. From this and other studies carried out, it seems that most children, provided always that the necessary physical and emotional stability is there, adjust themselves without difficulty to the fact that their mother goes out to work. Opinion polls among school children have shown that by and large they do not mind whether or not their mother works, provided she is at home when they return from school.

Employers are now doing much more to make this possible. They may allow the married woman to choose her own hours of work. They may encourage her to 'twin' with another worker so that between the two of them they cover a full-time job. By far the most imaginative scheme is 'flexitime', which offers greater choice in working hours. A woman can choose the hours she works and fit them in with family commitments and sudden emergencies at home. Provided she works the required hours per week or month, she can fit them in any time that the business is open. Sometimes she may decide to come in late; at others to leave early; and she may be allowed to accumulate hours so that she can take several days off without loss of pay or dismissal.

One of the main disadvantages for the married woman who works is that she has very little leisure time. The normal times for leisure, such as evenings and weekends, become occupied with household jobs. It is then that she does the laundry, cleans the house, cooks, does the family mending and any other things that need her attention. In fact, Michael Young and Peter Willmott, in their book *The Symmetrical Family,* point out that in modern society, where both husband and wife have full-time jobs, there is very little time for real leisure, except on holiday. This could do a great deal of harm, both physically and mentally, to people in such a situation.

Of course, part of the solution lies in a far greater use of modern equipment in the home, of packaged and pre-cooked foods, of disposable household linen, crockery and even clothes. Continental quilts, for example, can save much time and energy in bed-making. But these labour-saving devices are by no means the complete answer. It is also necessary to introduce much more order and planning into the home and its organisation, so that time and energy do not have to be spent on deciding what to do next, and so that any other member of the family can take over temporarily if the mother is unwell or otherwise incapacitated. Even so, the use of numerous labour-saving devices can, in some people, produce a sense of guilt. They feel they should be doing more themselves in looking after the home. An American experiment, for instance, showed how a well-known cake mix doubled its sales when it was suggested that an egg should be added to the mixture before baking.

Leisure Activities
What people do with their leisure time depends very much on their tastes, their income group, their own age and that of their family, and their health and strength. Young people will enjoy primitive and hazardous conditions which the older person would not even contemplate. The wealthy will pay heavily for something unusual, while the bookworm will bury himself in the public library. Yet there are certain things, like television, which appeal to almost everyone.

Ninety-four per cent of British families have television sets, most of them colour. Families on an average watch television for nineteen hours a week, and this seems to be fairly evenly spread throughout the income groups. Television is also a great pleasure to those who are elderly, sick or handicapped, for it provides them with an interest that takes them out of themselves. Others who make great use of television are children. For them it is a means of seeing a world with which they are not familiar, and of following exciting stories which they would have previously read in books.

The impact of television on young people has caused considerable consternation, particularly as twenty hours per week is given as the average viewing time for children. The main fear is that watching scenes of violence may frighten children and lead young people to adopt similar behaviour. Several assessments of the effects of such programmes on children have been made without any conclusive proof. The more sensitive child may possibly be frightened, but children on the whole do not seem to be unduly influenced. Cases have appeared in the newspapers of attempted murder by young people using a method seen on a television programme, but these are rare instances from among millions of viewers.

The most important social effect of television has been to encourage people to spend more of their leisure time in the home. This has indirectly caused them to make the home more comfortable to live in. But it has also led to a decline in attendance at live shows, such as theatres, concerts and cinemas, and many public houses have introduced meals and various forms of entertainment to try to keep their customers.

Other important home-based leisure activities are gardening, home decoration and repairs, and car cleaning and maintenance. Many of these arise from the fact that personal services are becoming so expensive. 'Do-it-yourself' includes almost anything from structural improvements, such as building an extension, to decorating, painting, wall-papering and home furnishing. With the use of the many new synthetic materials, this work has become far easier for the amateur to do, and it can be made to look so attractive that it is hardly distinguishable from professional work.

The rapid rise in prices has also led to a greater interest in gardening, particularly the growing of one's own vegetables. Similarly, home dressmaking and entertaining at home are beginning to replace buying clothes in shops and eating out in restaurants. Inviting friends home for a meal usually means more elaborate cooking than usual.

Visiting friends and relatives is the most important activity outside the home. Visiting relatives is far more common in the lower income groups because relatives tend to live fairly close and this makes visiting easy; it can be accomplished in a day or an afternoon. Entertaining friends and business colleagues is more prevalent among professional people and usually takes the form of a lunch or evening meal. Visiting is encouraged by the fact that most families now have a car and can drive the thirty miles or so which may be involved in a friendly call.

Eating out was very popular before prices began to rise so steeply. This was because most families had a margin of income which they could spend on food that was different and more attractive than that cooked at home. It was also made necessary by the lack of domestic help, particularly in a household where the wife was out at work. Today pre-cooked foods and facilities for buying ready-made meals are becoming much more common. There is also reasonably cheap home equipment for keeping food cooked in advance warm and ready for serving. This makes it possible for more entertaining to be done at home.

Sport is a popular form of leisure occupation, though participation in active sport is not so usual as it was a decade or so ago. Tennis, golf, riding, fishing and skating used to be confined to the higher income groups, but with public provision for these activities they have become far more widespread. On the other hand, many people now prefer to watch professional sport on television at home rather than take part in amateur games.

Some people like to spend their spare time doing voluntary work, like visiting old people or helping with a youth club. Others attend evening classes or join 'keep-fit' or yoga groups. Young people may spend their evenings dancing, playing darts or billiards in the pub, or even just sitting and talking. There is a very wide variety of ways of filling in the leisure hours and few people have exactly the same ideas about what they like to do.

Most people have two or three weeks' holiday a year which they spend in various ways, from a holiday cruise to a visit to a relative or friend. It is only comparatively recently that families have been able to go away in this manner. All that working people had as holidays a hundred years ago was some four bank holidays a year. The building of the railways and cheap excursion tickets enabled them to go to the seaside or into the country for the day, but they rarely went further afield.

Today, about half the families who go away for their holiday go abroad, Spain and Majorca being the most popular destinations. A very large proportion of these families will join a package tour, both because of its relative cheapness and because most of the arrangements are made in advance for them. The British Tourist Authority publishes an annual survey on holidaymaking which gives details of how holidays are spent, both abroad and in this country.

Many people are content to take their holidays in Britain, and with the fall in the value of the pound, an increasing number are likely to do so in future. Some of the more well-to-do may stay in hotels and guest houses, but with the rise in the price of accommodation, many more families are taking self-catering apartments, living in a caravan or camping. Most families use their car for transport, leaving rail travel for the elderly or the young who do not own a car or a motor bike.

The West Country is the most favoured area for holidays, although where a family goes depends very much on the age of the children. Younger children usually want the seaside, but as children grow older they may prefer mountain climbing or walking on the moors, bird-watching or fishing. Towns are becoming more popular as holiday centres, probably because the local authorities are taking more interest in publicising and displaying what may be of interest to tourists. This is particularly the case with foreign tourists, who seem to prefer to stay in the towns rather than the country, and to make excursions to nearby places of interest.

Yet about one-fifth of the adult population take no holiday away from home and many of them have not been away for several years. They spend their holidays decorating the house, working in the garden and watching television. Some probably prefer this, but many cannot afford anything else, particularly with the present high unemployment figures and high prices. Many of those who do not take holidays away from home are older people, and this is not always because they cannot afford to do so; they often dislike the upheaval of going away and all the arrangements that have to be made.

Leisure Industries

Industries have developed to cater for these many and various leisure activities. Some, like tourist agencies, are entirely involved in supplying the needs of leisure. Others make the needs of leisure activities their main aim, but possibly combine this with some similar form of production. In the case of motor vehicles, the majority are for pleasure, but the motor industry also produces lorries and vans. Broadcast programmes are largely for pleasure, but some, like those of the Open University, are educational.

In the past, leisure industries, if they could be so called, were largely the public houses and music halls. The provision of other leisure activities like museums, public parks and free lending libraries had to be undertaken by the State. This was because the middle class, who were the main source of private provision, did not think that the workers needed any special leisure activities. They considered that working people should work hard and rest when they were not working.

Since then the situation has changed enormously. The amount of leisure time has greatly increased and so has the money spent on leisure activities. Even since 1970, money spent on recreation and entertainment has increased by one-third, though with the present economic crisis this growth is slackening. It is difficult to say what proportion of the national expenditure goes on leisure activities because the figures are hidden under a variety of headings, but it is thought that it could be as great as 20 per cent. The result is that commercial leisure undertakings have greatly increased in size and number.

Critics of the leisure industries say that they aim to make people passive spectators of what is being provided in preference to doing things for themselves; for example, watching a football match rather than taking part in it, or going on a holiday which has been planned for them rather than one which they have organised for themselves. The critics also say that the mass market operates to standardise people's tastes and interests so that there is very little room for any initiative. On the other hand, by catering for a diversity of tastes, the leisure industries give genuine pleasure and satisfaction to a very large number of people, and through mass production they are able to offer many types of recreation and amusement, such as safari tours, for instance, which would otherwise be outside most people's income range.

The two largest organisations which provide for leisure are broadcasting and tourism, and in both cases there is a certain amount of government subvention. The British Broadcasting Corporation, which provides the four radio programmes, the television channels BBC 1 and BBC 2, and various local stations, has governors who are appointed by the Crown and financed by revenue from the annual television licence fees. The Independent Television Authority (ITA) is a commercial organisation, responsible for its own programmes which it finances largely through advertisements. The purpose of these two organisations is to entertain and at the same time to see that cultural and educational needs are met.

Tourism is largely the concern of private companies which compete with one another in offering attractive and reasonably priced holidays for different income groups, from the expensive world cruise to the camping holiday. The function of the British Tourist Authority, created by the government in 1969, is primarily to see that holidaymakers in this country, both British and foreign, are well received and have the best facilities that can be provided. It also provides up-to-date information about foreign countries.

Tourism and broadcasting are supported by various industries which provide, among their other products, some of the equipment that is needed. Much tourism requires the motor car, the aircraft or the coach, and broadcasting is supplemented by the record player and the cassette recorder. Similarly, taking part in active sports requires sports equipment, even if it is only football boots; do-it-yourself needs easily accessible DIY shops; and needlework and knitting depend on the supplies of the materials required. Reading, which is becoming an increasingly important leisure activity, is closely linked with the publishing industry and very much depends on the production of cheap and interesting paperbacks.

Meeting other people occupies a great deal of the leisure time of most people. This more often than not takes place at home, though it may involve going round to the local club or public house, or an evening out at a theatre or concert. In any case it is usually accompanied by a drink or two, on which the total expenditure has climbed continuously in recent years. This has stimulated the growth of breweries and similar industries.

Social clubs range from the expensive city club to the working man's social club and they provide a whole range of leisure activities from a well-equipped reading room to a snooker table. They were usually started in a small way by a group of congenial people, and continue to be managed by their members.

Some clubs, however, are encouraged by outside people who may both start and run them. Examples of these are youth clubs and clubs for the elderly. In both these cases the people who benefit from them are not in a financial position either to start and equip the premises or to keep them going. Voluntary organisations are usually formed for the purpose, although the members are often given some share in the management of the club. The State on the whole prefers voluntary organisations to do this, partly because it relieves the Exchequer of some of the expense, and partly because it considers that voluntary organisations are more suited to this sort of activity.

But the State will usually give grants and will help to advise and co-ordinate the services. Thus the Youth Service, which has existed since 1939, is a semi-government body, largely organised at county level, which brings together various leisure occupations for young people. Many national voluntary youth organisations like the Scouts, are linked with it. They may receive grants towards their work, but they are free to run themselves and decide their own lines of policy. Smaller local organisations, such as the church youth club, may depend entirely on their own resources. Where there are educational activities involved, the local education authorities may help, and in some cases they maintain their own youth clubs. Young Farmers' clubs are a good example of combining both social and educational activities. Because young people in farming today have to take a great deal of responsibility at an early age, they need not only leisure activities but also an opportunity to learn more about their work. This is provided by their clubs.

Some forms of leisure occupation, like drama, music and the arts, would find it difficult to continue without State support. Cultural activities such as these are costly to maintain and if they charged the public enough to cover their expenses, many people who might like to attend would be unable to do so. The Arts Council, which came into being more than a quarter of a century ago, helps to support a large number of orchestras and theatre companies, including the National Theatre and the Royal Shakespeare Theatre, and so makes it possible for the less well off to enjoy cultural activities which otherwise they would not be able to afford.

Planning for Leisure
Recent figures published by the Central Statistical Office in *Social Trends*, show that the amount of time left to people after work is on the increase. The average number of hours worked each week has fallen, particularly among male manual workers, who are working on an average a full two hours less than in 1972, even after overtime. The number of retired persons has increased by more than 600,000, those working part-time by nearly a million, and more than three-quarters of the population are now entitled to at least three weeks' paid holiday a year. Some of this increase in leisure time is, of course, due to lack of employment, but there is no doubt that whatever the future may bring, people are going to have more free time to fill themselves. It is therefore very important that they should have some idea of what to do with it.

Looking at the situation from a long-term point of view, the place where such help should begin is in the schools, so that when young people leave school they are aware of the need to have interests outside their work. The Newsom Committee tried to encourage the growth of extra-curricular activities which would widen the horizons of interest and enjoyment and sharpen a person's perception and discrimination. Liberal and social studies, arts and crafts and physical skills have been provided for many years by the schools, though these have concentrated more on how to do things rather than on how to organise leisure time. They emphasise the teaching of a skill rather than cultivate an enjoyment in what is being done.

Some schools try to help their pupils to make their own decisions about the ways in which they spend their time by encouraging initiative. This is sometimes connected with the Outward Bound movement, which tests a young person's resourcefulness, physical fitness and endurance in mountain climbing, rescue operations and other forms of adventurous activity. Most schools have a rather more ordinary approach, and arrange children's cruises and trips abroad so that pupils can learn about and visit places of interest. Similarly, they may be taken to concerts, art galleries and theatres or encouraged to look at the more informative documentaries on television.

In many cases it is only as an adult that a person begins to be aware of the need to plan for leisure time. He or she may by then have experienced some of the loneliness and isolation of free time away from home in the anonymity of a large city, or lack of acceptance in a closed village community. The need at this stage is for some absorbing interest or hobby which will fill spare time.

This is what most of the adult centres and colleges are trying to do. They are not concentrating as much as they did on further vocational training or academic learning aimed at improving career prospects. But they are offering vocational courses with a closer application to 'living'. These include such things as flower-arranging, antique-buying, party-giving and exotic cooking. They are taught in a way which places the subject in its wider context and arouses the student's personal interest and ingenuity.

Since a great deal of leisure time is spent in or near the home, it is essential that the house and its surroundings should encourage the pursuit of leisure occupations. This means that there should be space, privacy and warmth. Now that most households have a television set and do much of their entertaining at home, the main living room has gained a new importance. It must be big enough for these purposes and adequately heated. This will often be by some form of central heating, although in older houses a solid fuel fire may have to suffice with some background heating.

There needs to be space elsewhere for homework, hobbies and perhaps record playing, and this can be difficult in the smaller modern houses and flats. Noise can be a problem, especially if the design is open plan, or if there is little sound-proofing between rooms.

As for space outside the house, the coalshed has already given way to the fuel oil-tank or been converted to enlarge the capacity of the house. Space is also needed for parking the car and tinkering with it, for children's play equipment and for pets, as well as for the growing number of caravans and boats which families now own. The exodus of families from the densely populated areas of the towns to council and other estates on the periphery has helped to fulfil these desires for space and comfort.

Outside the home, local authorities are encouraging various forms of leisure activity through a more creative use of open spaces. They are providing hard, all-weather surfaces for sport, with clubhouses that have modern changing rooms and toilets and other facilities such as bars, lounges and rooms for family use. Indoor swimming pools and sports halls in the larger towns are becoming more usual, and where these are too expensive to build, a more imaginative use of existing halls, churches and public houses is being encouraged, so that plays, music, folk-singing and exhibitions can be organised.

Far greater attention is being given to helping families enjoy their holidays. The British Tourist Authority has not only encouraged a rapid growth in hotel building, extension and improvement, it has also brought about some changes in the types of accommodation available. The swing is towards the more informal, self-catering accommodation such as holiday flats, chalets, caravans and camp sites, where water is laid on and some provision made for everyday shopping requirements.

Visitors are being encouraged to see and do the things a particular area has to offer. The local tourist office used to do little beyond supply information about what could be seen and done in the district. Now scenic views are being opened up so that the occupants of cars can have a view of the countryside. Historic houses and gardens are allowing the public in on certain days, castles are being restored and wild life parks created. This is combined with the availability of active sports, like fishing, sailing, canoeing, skiing, pony trekking and climbing on a much wider scale and at a cost which is within the range of a far greater number of people. All this requires a certain degree of co-operation between the Department of the Environment, the local authorities and semi-voluntary organisations like the National Trust.

The Department of the Environment is the successor to the Ministry of Works which used to superintend the royal buildings and other ancient monuments, and which is now responsible for the preservation of the amenities of the countryside and of historic towns, the care of coastal districts and the control of pollution. This wider range of activity has meant that it is far easier for the Department and the local authority to work together in developing the amenities and resources of an area.

Large areas of natural beauty as well as many historic and interesting buildings are owned by the National Trust. Since it is an organisation incorporated by Parliament but independent of the State, it relies for its finances on the voluntary support of private individuals, particularly those who join the Trust and for the cost of their membership get free admission to its numerous buildings and gardens.

Many other historic buildings have been accepted by the Treasury in lieu of death duties. The owners are often allowed to continue to live in part of them, and they recoup some of their maintenance expenses from the entrance fees paid by visitors. This encourages them to provide attractive services, including refreshments and sometimes the freedom of the grounds for picnics.

Much more care is now taken both by the Department of the

Environment and the National Trust in the preparation of their leaflets and books on the history and content of their properties. They are bought and read widely with the result that the public are becoming far better informed about, and much more interested in, the places they visit. An increasing number of people are going to see such places, and local newspapers often contain a list of properties and gardens in the area with their opening times.

Now that visiting historic houses and museums is so popular, coach tours are arranged to take people to them, knowledgeable and interesting guides show the visitors round, and modern methods of display are used for articles of interest. Now that there is less money to spend on holidays, well-equipped caravans are being designed and put on the market, more caravan and camping sites are being made available, with modern sanitation and perhaps a shop supplying basic groceries. Dangerous outdoor sports, like pot-holing, have gained in popularity and this means more attention to safety measures to prevent accidents. Those who are planning for our leisure have to be on the alert not only for changes in people's tastes, but for all the other factors which may affect what people choose to do with their spare time.

5 Housing the Family

Shelter, like food and clothing, is one of the essentials of life. But housing involves a good deal more than a roof over one's head. There should be enough room for the family to live satisfactorily and happily together; a water supply which is adequate for the family's needs; sufficient heating and lighting for the home to be comfortable to live in; and adequate cooking facilities, and enough storage space.

All this is complicated by the fact that once houses are built they last for a long time, and since they are expensive to build it is not usually economic to pull them down once they are out of date and replace them with more modern ones. The alternative is to modernise and this, too, can be costly. In Britain today much of the housing stock dates from the turn of the century and unless steps are taken to repair the older houses and bring them up to contemporary standards they run the risk of turning into slums.

The Development of a Housing Policy
It is only since the First World War that the government has intervened on any scale in the provision of housing. Before this the supply of houses was determined almost entirely by what individual people felt was needed. When England was an agricultural country it was the duty of the squire or farmer to provide a cottage for his labourers. This he did in a variety of ways, the most usual being the 'tied' cottage which was made available to the agricultural labourer for as long as he worked for a particular farmer. The difficulty of this arrangement was that when the labourer retired or changed his employment he at once became homeless. Legislation is in process to give the agricultural labourer greater security of tenure.

Similarly, towns developed in a haphazard manner, with new houses being built by the inhabitants as they were needed. Those who made money would build themselves a new house, selling their older, more dilapidated property to newcomers from the country. Such houses would usually fall into a bad state of repair and were often very overcrowded, with a family of eight or so packing themselves into 'one up and one down'. The industrial development of the late eighteenth and early nineteenth centuries aggravated the situation, and many families found themselves living in the most appalling conditions in the new industrial towns. Instead of having houses provided by their employers as had been the case in the country, they had to make their own arrangements and pay exorbitant rents for the poorest of accommodation. Thus it became a profitable business to own, let and sub-let such houses. House property came to be regarded as a commercial investment likely to yield a high return. A row of dwellings belonging to some landlord called Mr Smith would be named 'Smith's Rents' and tenants would be charged as much as the market would bear, with little regard to the fact that they were paying an excessive proportion of their income for very poor accommodation.

Most of the houses built at this time for working people were badly constructed. They were terraced houses, built 'back-to-back' with ventilation on one side only and no facilities for sanitation or water supply. The cheapest materials were used and as many as possible crowded into a given area. Some of these houses can still be seen in the very poor areas of our towns and cities where rehousing schemes have not yet been put into effect.

On the other hand there were many conscientious landlords and honest builders of small houses. They included the housing trusts which built tenements for the so-called 'industrious' classes. The earlier ones were mostly charitable trusts, but the later ones were often financed by industrialists like Peabody and Guinness. Most of these tenements were massive blocks of flats built to a high density, and some of them are still being used after more than a hundred years. In their day they were regarded as models of their kind, although they provided only one room per family with a cold water tap and a lavatory on each floor. Today, in spite of many improvements, they appear very drab. But they serve to indicate the great advances that have been made in working class housing in the last hundred years.

The Royal Commission on the Housing of the Working Classes pointed out in 1885 that private enterprise and charitable trusts could never keep pace with the demands for housing. Therefore it suggested that local authorities should help a resident occupier to buy his house if he wanted to, and should also build houses themselves for the lower income groups. But very few local authorities used these powers and little improvement was made on the massed slums in the towns and the tumble-down cottages of the countryside. Even by the end of the First World War a commission in Scotland found that one-quarter of the population lived in 'single-ends', which consisted of one room with a single window.

Peace in 1918 gave rise to a great wave of enthusiasm for better conditions. Parliament and the country alike were determined to build houses 'fit for heroes to live in'. But the cost of labour had increased greatly and the cost of materials had soared, so that local authorities were reluctant to involve themselves in schemes which could lead to heavy financial losses. It was not until the late twenties that the cost

An example of the slum conditions still to be found in some of the poorest urban areas

of building began to fall and an increasing number of houses were constructed by both the local authorities and private enterprise. Over one million council houses were built for renting in the period between the two world wars and more than twice this number, mostly for sale, were built by private enterprise. This meant that, with the drop in the price of building, a substantial number of better-paid families were able to buy their own homes. They did this with loans from the building societies. Had there not been a second world war, this housing policy might have met the needs of all but the worst areas of the large cities. As it was, many homes were demolished by the bombing and others fell into a state of disrepair, so that by the end of the war housing was again in short supply and so very expensive.

At the end of the Second World War it became obvious that something needed to be done. Many young couples, most of whom had married during the war, wanted homes of their own. So emergency housing – the 'prefabs' – were put up by the government on a large scale, often on bomb sites. Although the prefabs were not aesthetically attractive, they had reasonable standards of living space and, for the first time in houses constructed by the government, they contained much of the labour-saving equipment which up until then had been the prerogative of the higher income groups.

Since about one-third of all houses in Britain were damaged to a greater or lesser extent during the Second World War, and of these more than 300,000 were totally destroyed, the authorities had to increase greatly the amount of subsidised council housing if they were to provide enough homes. So they built new housing estates on the outskirts of the towns, and 'New Towns', to which people were encouraged to move from the large cities to become part of a self-contained township where they both lived and worked.

The government now began to recognise that good housing was a social need which it had to supply, not only for the poorer people but for other income groups as well. Therefore, as well as subsidising council housing, it began to encourage private housing by granting permits for building, for the acquisition of land and for the availability of materials. This tended to help the higher rather than the lower income families, but it did have the effect of reducing competition for existing lower priced houses and so made them more widely available to those who could not afford to pay very much.

A government housing policy has in the first instance to take into account the number of people to be housed. But it is not only the number of individuals that matters; there is also the question of whether they are willing to live together. A family of parents and young children are usually willing to do so. But single people, the widowed, the divorced and the elderly often like to live on their own. Therefore it is the structure of the population that is important in terms of housing. That means the size and age grouping of families and the expected number of single, married or divorced people. Small, unexpected changes in these groupings can drastically alter planning policy.

Even then it is the household rather than the family that determines what housing is needed. Generally speaking a household is regarded as a group of people who take their meals together, whether or not they are related, and this includes lodgers in some households. On the other hand it might mean one person living alone who is responsible for his or her own housekeeping. In an industrial society like ours the majority of families do have separate households. While single people may live with others when they are young they often set up house on their own when they reach middle age. The widowed, divorced or elderly, on the other hand, may set up house on their own to begin with, but later may go to live with other people.

Each household usually occupies a single dwelling – an accommodation unit with its own front door. But often in the older areas of the towns several households have to occupy one dwelling and share some of its facilities such as the bathroom or the kitchen. They may have their own front door, but have to pass through some part of the accommodation of another household to get to it. This is often the case with families in the lower income ranges who are unable to afford anything better, particularly young couples who find it difficult to get any other accommodation when they marry.

Various other factors affect the sort of housing demanded, particularly social class and the size of the family income. Housing takes up quite a large proportion of family expenditure and so, as income rises, families are likely to be more selective as to the sort of housing they require. Privacy and space are at a premium in the middle and upper classes. When incomes are low families may be willing to put up with the many inconveniences of the older house, but as income rises they want all that modern housing can provide. There is not, therefore, a single housing market where demand can be related to supply, but many different, specialised markets where the needs of different groups of people have to be met.

Social change can also affect the housing situation, for as the general standard of living rises more and more families want their own homes. Young married couples are no longer willing to live with their parents for a while. Close relatives like grandparents, uncles and aunts, may live near other members of the family rather than with them and in independent households of their own. Wealthier people may now have two households, a flat in the city and a country or weekend cottage. Students may have two homes – their parents' house and a flat near their college. With the increase in unemployment, men who cannot find work locally may leave their family in their existing accommodation and themselves go to a place where they can find a job. Here they may live in furnished apartments, feeding themselves and so counting as another household.

Economic factors can also play a part, especially the relative ease with which money can be acquired to purchase property. Most property is purchased with the aid of a loan from a building society or from some individual or institution in the form of a private mortgage. In both cases the prevailing rate of interest has to be paid, and the worse the economic conditions are, the higher this is likely to be. The difference between a loan from a building society and a loan from a private source lies in the method of repayment. With a building society, the payments which are made by the borrower at monthly intervals represent both interest and capital. This goes on until all the capital has been repaid. With a private loan, interest only is paid periodically, and the capital may be paid off in part or whole at any time, according to the arrangement made between lender and borrower.

Property is either held in absolute or permanent ownership, which is known as freehold, or for a fixed period of time, after which it returns to its original owner, in which case it is said to be leasehold. The owner of freehold property holds the title deeds, which have to be handed over to the new owner if the property is sold. A leaseholder has to pay the owner for the privilege of using his property, and the sum which he has to pay periodically is known as 'rent'. He enters into a contract with his landlord as to the length of time of the lease, the amount of rent to be paid, and any other outgoings for which he (the leaseholder) is responsible, and if he does not keep to the terms of his contract, the owner may terminate the lease.

The Present Housing Situation

The present housing stock can be divided into owner-occupied houses, many of them large and well equipped; council houses, which are a fairly uniform group and reasonably well equipped; privately rented houses which are often among the worst in the country; and furnished accommodation which is very variable but only represents some 2 per cent of the total stock.

Much of this stock of houses is relatively old. Forty-six per cent of houses in Greater London were built before 1919 and some 30 per cent between the two world wars. The situation is even worse in Scotland where there are large numbers of houses going back to before the 1880s, most of them in Glasgow and Edinburgh. In the rest of Britain the situation is slightly better. These older buildings lack many of the basic amenities like main drainage and a hot water supply. But many

Housing the Family

of them are solidly built and can be modernised if it is possible to raise the money to do so.

Most people in the lower income groups live in rented property owned either by private landlords or by the local council. Private landlords own much of the older stock of houses for, as we have seen, investment in such property was very popular in the nineteenth century. It was not only the small landlord who might own a row of terrace houses or a small number of cottages. Big landlords like the Duke of Bedford and the Church Commissioners owned large parts of the poorer areas of the cities and rented out the accommodation.

Much of this rented accommodation is no longer available, either because it has been replaced by more up-to-date building, or because the cost of repairs has proved too much for the landlord, who has sold it. Sometimes the new owner might convert the property into furnished accommodation. It could then consist of small units with the tenants sharing most of the essential equipment with their neighbours. This is particularly the case in the London area and in other large cities where the prospective tenants may be either students or young clerical workers who are away from home for the first time, short-term and temporary residents looking for other accommodation, or overseas visitors in Britain for a short stay.

Another reason for the decline in the sector of privately rented houses was the introduction of rent control during the First World War. The government fixed a ceiling rent in order to divert resources from housing to defence and to prevent the scarcity of houses from driving up their price. Even when the war was over some control was continued to prevent rents from rising beyond the means of the lower income groups, and controlled tenancies have continued in a modified form up to the present. An important result has been that many landlords have not received enough rent to enable them to undertake necessary repairs on their property.

The situation is intensified today by recent legislation in favour of the tenant which makes it very difficult to get vacant possession of both furnished and unfurnished property unless it is needed by the owner as his sole place of residence, or the rent is continually in arrears. Many landlords are not willing to tie up their property in this way, and once it becomes vacant they put it on the market.

The effect of all this has been greatly to reduce the amount of privately rented property on the market. At the same time it has discouraged owners from making their property available for letting, particularly those who in the past would have done so for short-term tenancies. This is making it much more difficult for students to find accommodation, and for the unemployed to move temporarily to a place where they might be able to find a job.

One of the best examples of modern council housing: the Lillington Gardens council estate in Pimlico, south London

The alternative form of rented accommodation is council housing, much of which is modern and well equipped. The building of council housing dates from the 1920s, with a big increase after the Second World War, so that by the sixties those who lived in council houses were far more numerous than those who rented private accommodation.

Council housing has many attractions. It provides a family with a house of its own, usually with a garden and sometimes a garage or parking space. About one-fifth of the housing is in the form of maisonettes and flats which may suit those who have older children or are out at work all day. Such housing has, on the whole, a uniformly high standard with modern amenities and quite often central heating. The main drawback is size. Almost all the houses have only two or three bedrooms. This suits the average family, but the very large family as well as couples without children can find it difficult to obtain accommodation. They may have to turn to the privately rented sector to find what they want, or try to buy their own house. For a family which has no house to sell and cannot afford the deposit demanded by a building society the situation may be critical.

With the increase in council housing, the care and management of council housing estates has become a large-scale operation and a highly important responsibility of local government. Although the central government issues general advice and guidance, it is the local councils who run the estates.

In letting their houses, local authorities are under a statutory obligation to re-house families who are displaced as a result of slum clearance. They are also required to give preference to families living in overcrowded or otherwise unsatisfactory conditions. This will mean the selection of applications from a waiting list, and for this purpose most councils use a points scheme to assess the comparative housing requirements of the applicants. Areas vary greatly in the length of their waiting lists; in some it may be a long time before the council can house a family, while elsewhere this may be done comparatively quickly.

Rents are normally collected weekly at the door of the house, although in recent years there has been a steady increase in the number of tenants who pay their rents directly to the town hall, probably because they would be at work when the collector called. The collector frequently undertakes other management duties, such as dealing with tenants' inquiries and requests for repairs. The council used to be responsible for all repairs, but many authorities are now transferring the responsibility for internal decoration and minor internal repairs to the tenant.

Housing management covers other things: seeing that the conditions of tenancy are observed, the care of the house and the garden, dealing with trouble between tenants, and with applications by tenants for transfer or exchange. It may also involve legal advice and putting the tenant in touch with one of the social services. The pioneer in this field was Octavia Hill (1838-1912) who from her early girlhood worked among the poor of London. Horrified by the neglected houses she visited, she succeeded, with the help of her friend John Ruskin, in establishing herself as a landlady in a slum area in Marylebone. By personally collecting the rents, carrying out repairs and offering advice on a wide variety of matters, she was able to bring about some improvement. This encouraged her to involve others and to introduce a method of managing property on weekly or short-term tenancies. Her managers were trained not only in the collection of rents, but also in assessing and dealing with repairs and in the various problems of welfare. This led ultimately to the formation of the Society of Housing Managers which seeks to maintain standards in this form of work.

Local councils soon realised that efficient management as well as the happiness of their tenants depended to a large extent on the employment of a fully trained and qualified staff. By 1926 trained housing managers were being employed in the housing departments of the larger local authorities, and since then local councils have usually seen that they have adequate housing management. Housing management is not confined to council housing. It may be used by any large landlord, such as some of the commissions owning an amount of small rented property.

At the same time as council housing was increasing, a great growth in owner-occupation was taking place. Between 1919 and 1960 some four and a half million private houses were built, and this growth has continued. The result has been that about a quarter of all houses are now owner-occupied. Many of them are highly valued properties in the more desirable suburbs. The older houses are large, but the modern ones are usually smaller, with a garden, a double garage, and modern amenities. Such houses are a good deal more luxurious than those provided by the councils. Typical examples are the terraces of 'town houses'.

The rise in relative incomes has brought house purchase within the range of a much larger number of people. They are able to raise the difference between the amount they can borrow from a building society or other source and the selling price, to pay the legal costs of transferring the property (or conveyancing), and to afford or undertake themselves the repairs which may be needed for old property. Where the local council permits, some people are buying their own council houses.

Occasionally those who find it difficult to raise all the money required to purchase their own house may do so in co-operation with others. Various schemes of co-operative management and shared ownership are being tried out. A group of people can borrow money more easily and since they know one another they can ensure that each regularly pays up what he has agreed to contribute. This could become an important way of meeting the decline in the number of houses available for private renting.

Housing Standards
It is necessary not only that the family should be housed, but that the housing provided should reach a certain standard of quality and comfort. Very little attention was given to these things before the First World War. But in 1917 a committee was set up under the chairmanship of Sir John Tudor-Walters to consider the question of housing standards for working class dwellings. The committee recommended that every house should have a living room, a room for cooking, washing up and other domestic purposes and a minimum floor space. It also restricted the density of house building to not more than twelve houses to the acre. Although the recommended standards were subsequently trimmed down, the report of the committee did result in a marked improvement in the layout and quality of houses.

Criticism of the continuing low standards, and speculation as to the likely long-term effect on the housing stock, led to the Parker-Morris report, *Homes for Today and Tomorrow,* published in 1961. The committee responsible for the report took into account the greater variety of leisure pursuits, the increasing use of labour-saving equipment, and the need for members of the family to have facilities for quiet study. They recommended an overall increase in space standards and adequate heating so that maximum use could be made of available floor space, and dwellings could be more adaptable to family needs. This report represents a landmark in the approach to housing standards and is important in that it applies to all types of housing, not just that of the lower income groups.

The majority of owner-occupied houses are reasonably well equipped, though increasing concern is being expressed at the poor quality of some of the new private building compared with that of council housing. There is, however, an appreciable number of owner-occupied houses, usually in areas which have deteriorated, which are old and very badly serviced. Such houses may have no hot water supply, few of them have a bath or else it has to be shared with another household, and overcrowding may be prevalent.

In council housing essential plumbing and kitchen equipment is provided, except in a small number of older houses which the council may have purchased for improvement or demolition. One difficulty with council housing is adjusting the number of people to the size of the house. When a family grows or diminishes in size the council will usually move it to more appropriate accommodation. But this is not always available, especially if the family is larger or smaller than average. Nor is the council tenant always willing to move when asked to do so. While the average family moves about every seven years, the family in a council house stays a good deal longer.

From the point of view of amenities, privately rented houses present the worst picture. Half of them have no bath, two-fifths have no hot water supply and one-fifth have no flush toilet or have to share one with others. On the other hand this sector of housing has an asset which the country cannot afford to lose: a very varied supply of accommodation ranging from the furnished room to the large Victorian house. Thus it can meet the needs of those who do not easily fit into the council housing schemes. If these houses in the private sector could be modernised and occupied by the people who need them, we would go a long way towards solving our housing problem.

Recent legislation has tried to encourage this. In the first place it is necessary to decide whether such property is capable of repair, or whether it must be considered unfit for habitation. Much of it is structurally sound, but it does not have modern amenities and may have been neglected for some time. The Housing Act of 1957 lays down conditions for determining whether a property is fit for habitation. It takes into account the stability of the building, state of repair, freedom from damp, natural lighting, ventilation, water supply, drainage and sanitary conveniences, and facilities for storage, the preparation and cooking of food, and the disposal of waste water. A house is said to be unfit for human habitation if any one of these facilities is so defective that it makes the house unsuitable for occupation.

Not all unfit houses have to be demolished. They can be modernised with the aid of government improvement grants, which mean that the owner only has to meet part of the cost. These grants have been available since the later 1940s and, in general, consist of two types, standard and discretionary grants. Standard grants were first introduced with the House Purchase and Housing Acts of 1959. They are available for the provision of the four standard amenities – internal water closet, bath and wash-basin, kitchen sink and hot and cold water supply – as well as a satisfactory food store. If a local authority feels that the cost would be too high, it may permit a reduced standard which could exclude the wash-basin or bath; and where one or two of the amenities are already available a smaller grant will be provided for the provision of the others.

Discretionary grants are made under the 1969 Housing Act. They are not normally given unless the dwelling has a future life of about thirty years, and they can be paid for conversion as well as for improvement. They include grants towards additional items such as treating damp, providing a proper drainage system, adequate facilities for heating, fuel storage and cooking. Landlords can be compelled to undertake such improvements with grant aid if this is desired by a tenant, and provided the tenant is willing to pay a higher rent.

A bad environment may lead to houses being allowed to decay. Therefore it is not just houses that need to be improved, but the environment as well. The 1964 Housing Act gives powers to a local authority to declare an improvement area and to compel landlords to bring their property up to the standard amenity level. The basic purpose of this is to encourage local authorities to concern themselves not only with slum areas and council housing, but with all unsatisfactory residential areas.

In recent years there has been a definite shift towards more concern for those dwellings which are not so much unfit as unsatisfactory for people to live in, and this includes the question of environment as well as structure and equipment. A comprehensive overall plan is needed if this problem is to be dealt with adequately. The main difficulty is that unless the stock of housing increases, the improvement of one area leads to the obsolescence of another, and so any overall plan needs to be nation-wide.

At the moment shortage of money for housing is one of the government's biggest problems. It is therefore trying to steer what funds it has to the areas of greatest need. The general idea of the housing legislation of 1974 was for 'housing action areas' to be chosen for immediate relief. Such an area was to consist of a selected group of about 300 to 400 houses, half or more without baths, and probably containing the elderly, the poorer members of the community, families with special problems, the unemployed, and those with no permanent home. Such an area was to be brought up to standard, and when this was accomplished attention would be turned to another selected area.

Types of Houses
Houses take their character largely from the type of plan followed. House planning is influenced by a variety of factors, the most important of which is the amount of money available. It is impossible to build an original or an elaborate house cheaply. Houses for the smaller income groups have to be stereotyped in design, as in the case of prefabricated building.

The plan will be affected by the type of site, and by the availability of materials. Cottages in the Cotswolds are likely to be built in local stone, but bricks may be used for similar cottages in other areas. Fashion plays quite an important part. Le Corbusier, the Swiss architect, set the style for the numerous concrete buildings we have today.

The introduction of modern conveniences into the home has played a large part in determining house planning – the modern bathroom with its lavatory, wash-basin and bidet, central heating, a well-equipped kitchen and a solid garage. All these have increased the complexity of construction work and added materially to the costs, and so have indirectly reduced the size of houses.

The result is a wide variety in types of dwellings. There are terraced houses, semi-detached and detached houses, maisonettes and bungalows, high-rise flats and smaller apartment houses. Some contain a large number of rooms and others only a few; some have many amenities; others have few. Some types of accommodation are much more sought after than others, which forces up their price. In other words the market for certain types of housing, like the modern town house, is fairly exclusive.

The type of house a family wants depends very much on its economic and social situation. While housing is reckoned to take up quite a large part of the family income, there are limits beyond which a family is not prepared to go. The amount devoted to housing depends upon the scale of preferences, or priorities, of any particular family. Thus housing has to compete with things like food, clothing and perhaps education expenses for those who want to send their children to private schools.

The occupation of the head of the family can influence the choice of housing. If he has to live near his place of work, this may mean being in an area where property values are high, restricting the size and type of housing that he can afford. People frequently prefer to live near those with whom they have some things in common. Thus a family with young children usually prefers an area where there are other families with young children. So certain areas, probably in the suburbs, become essential for a particular family, and the choice of house available here may be restricted. Factors such as these play a less important part in council housing, where the size of the family is usually the deciding factor, and individual choice is somewhat limited.

The stage of life of family members also influences the type of house they require. Most people spend much of the first two decades of their life in their parents' home. When they leave home to take up some form of training, to find work or get married, they may live in small and ill-equipped rooms or flats which are close to their place of employment, but relatively expensive. When the first child is born their home becomes to an increasing extent the centre of the parents' lives. They need more privacy and storage space, a bath and plenty of hot water, a reasonably well-equipped kitchen and possibly a utility room. As the children grow older, separate sleeping accommodation is required and more play space becomes essential. Quite often a garden is wanted. At this stage couples become more active in their search for housing and more discriminating. So they tend to move fairly frequently both as the family grows up and with changes of job. The next stage is usually when the children are grown up and one of the parents dies. Then a choice has to be made between moving to a smaller house or bungalow, or living with relatives. Not everyone passes through all these stages. Those who do not marry may never move further than the first two or three stages, and some people insist on living in the relatively large family house until they die.

The most frequent movers are young people, provided they have managed to buy a house in the early years of marriage. They will have something to sell if they want to move, though the extent to which this will meet the cost of a new house will depend on whether they go to a more expensive area and on what they want to buy. But in any case they will have some sort of 'hedge' against changes in property values. Those who fail to buy when young may never get another opportunity, either because of the expense of a growing family or because by the time they are in their forties the opportunities of borrowing dwindle. This is just when people need good housing, and unless they have managed to get a council house, their chances of moving are poor.

Others who find housing particularly difficult are those who do not fit exactly into the prevailing pattern. There is a scarcity of housing for those with large families of teenagers who want a place where they can make as much noise as they like. Similarly there is very little suitable housing for single people with small incomes. This is particularly the case with students, many of whom find themselves confined to conversions, slums and rooms in substandard property.

One of the problems of moving is that in order to get what they want the family may have to go quite a distance. New schools, shops and friends have to be found and the father may have to change his job. A far greater variety in the design of individual houses in an area is needed so that families can remain within the area and move with the minimum upheaval. An alternative to this, one which is rare in this country, is greater flexibility in house design so that it is possible to alter the allocation of house space and use it for different purposes as the needs of the family change.

When redevelopment takes place in a large city like London, it usually means a completely new lay-out of buildings with as high a density as possible. The modern way of achieving this is by high blocks of flats with open spaces and better views than were possible with the rows of cottage-type homes of late Victorian times. When such high-rise dwellings were first built they were thought to be a good thing because amongst other things they offered better ventilation and views over the city. But many tenants have come to dislike them and in some cases they have been difficult to let.

There are various reasons for this. In the first place these massive concrete buildings can be fourteen or fifteen storeys high, and since they have been built only recently, little is known about their safety or their structural defects. Serious disasters, like that at Ronan Point in East London, when one whole side of a building collapsed, have led to questions being asked about their safety and to unwillingness among tenants to live in the higher storeys.

From the point of view of the tenants there are many practical difficulties. The lifts stop only at every other floor and are often out of order. This can cause much distress to old people and to mothers with young children. The lifts, like the long corridors opening onto the flats on each floor, are areas where a good deal of hooliganism takes place. There are constant complaints about excessive noise, inadequate insulation against the weather and undesirable neighbours. Young mothers cannot watch their children when they go down to play in the grounds since they may live several storeys up. The result is that some children are rarely allowed out. The only fresh air they get is on the small balconies which each flat has for drying washing and all the other things for which a yard is normally used.

Perhaps loneliness is the greatest social problem, for housewives no longer meet one another in the streets or over the garden fence. Some of them have no friends at all in the flats and no one to whom they can go in an emergency. They become afraid to go out, and yet feel shut in if they stay at home. Doctors and social workers can trace many psychological problems to this sort of housing.

Its main advantage is that it does provide suitable housing for single people and childless couples, although in the case of the elderly, their flats need to be on the ground floor. The general attitude now seems to be that accommodation of this nature is required, but that its height should be restricted. It is suggested that councils should build more houses and maisonettes for those who would prefer them, so that only those who like living in huge blocks of flats will have to do so.

Housing for Specialised Groups
Certain people in the community need special attention. Some are unable to afford the rent of suitable housing and so become homeless. Others, because of some particular disability, find it difficult to live in an ordinary house. Among them are the handicapped and the elderly.

For those who are too poor to pay the normal rent, local authorities may reduce what they charge for council accommodation. (This concession was extended to some private renting under the Housing Finance Act, 1972.) Leeds was the first local authority to do this, and now most councils have introduced differential rents. They usually take into account the income of their tenants and certain liabilities such as the illness of a member of the family, and the rent is reduced accordingly. In the private housing sector some families may be fortunate in finding a rent-controlled property. But most are faced with very high rents, and if they have not lived in the district very long, or have no children, they do not usually qualify for council housing. Immigrants who have just arrived in this country, and still have to find suitable employment, often come into this category, as well as an increasing number of single persons who have been made redundant and are seeking other employment.

Under the National Assistance Act, 1948, the local authorities are obliged to find temporary accommodation for families who become homeless. But it may involve separating husband and wife, since there is no statutory obligation to provide for the husband. He is expected to go out and find a job for himself, so that home life may be restored. Most local authorities provide such accommodation in large Victorian houses which have been converted into bed-sitting rooms. But the present scarcity of housing is so acute that they frequently have to offer bed and breakfast accommodation in private hotels. This can mean that the family has nowhere to go in the daytime.

The number of families applying for temporary accommodation has been steadily increasing, particularly in the inner London areas and the larger conurbations, for these are districts which attract people at risk, especially the poor, the unemployed, the immigrant, the transient and the young who have left home. These are also the areas with long waiting lists for council housing. The 1974 Rent Act, which brought security of tenure to tenants in furnished property, has helped to reduce the numbers of those evicted and so to prevent homelessness. But an increasing number of the homeless are single-parent families. In some cases the parents have started a family with little intention of staying together permanently. In others, marital disputes have resulted in separation or divorce.

A number of housing associations and trusts provide accommodation for the homeless and the Supplementary Benefits Commission has powers to make grants to selected voluntary organisations which do this. One such society, Shelter, is particularly outstanding for its hard-hitting publicity campaigns and its imaginative housing of families which are not attractive to local authorities or private landlords. CHAR, the Campaign for the Homeless and Roofless, concentrates on the single homeless. A growing number of these are young people who have lived in lodging houses and shelters, or have been discharged from prison or mental hospitals with no permanent place to go to.

Living in caravans, which used to be confined to gypsies and travellers, is now becoming a way of finding a relatively cheap home. Working married couples, some of them with children, have adopted this way of life because they have been unable to find anything else. Their chief difficulty is finding a suitable site, for there is considerable variation in facilities for water, sanitation, lighting and cooking. The Caravan Sites Act, 1968, has made it the duty of local authorities to provide regulated sites. But these are few in number and not always in convenient places, so that often families in caravans settle on illegal sites from which they are periodically removed. This can cause a good deal of disruption, especially to the children, who may have to be constantly changing schools and making new friends.

A number of disabled, elderly and handicapped people require special housing, if they are to remain in their own homes as long as possible. It is important that they should be close to friends and relatives in case they need help; and this may involve re-housing them. They must also be near shops and public transport if they are to lead a reasonably normal life. In addition, they require special equipment to enable them to do the ordinary household jobs. The Piercy Committee of 1956 pleaded that 'all those responsible for new local authority housing schemes should bear in mind the needs of the disabled. Some of the accommodation should be specially designed without steps and with wide doors to allow the passage of wheelchairs.' This was followed up in 1962 by an exhibition of purpose-built accommodation for the disabled. The result has been a growing awareness of their need for suitable housing and equipment.

While in hospital many disabled patients are taught to do ordinary domestic tasks, such as preparing a meal and washing up; and they are encouraged to practise what they have been taught before going home. Alterations in the home, are usually necessary as well, involving such things as putting up handrails, the raising of lavatories and the provision of ramps for a wheelchair. Hospitals and charities may help, but under the Chronically Sick Disabled Persons Act, 1970, local authorities have a duty to consider the special needs of the handicapped and disabled, to make adaptations to the home, and to see that the minimal equipment is provided. Many of them are fulfilling this duty readily. The disabled have their own magazine, *Responaut,* which contains many new ideas about ways in which they can be helped to live more normally, including various new gadgets and adaptations.

For the elderly, it is necessary to provide accommodation that is comfortable and warm, that reduces the amount of housework to a minimum and eliminates difficult steps and stairs and other hazards which can cause accidents. The desire for privacy needs to be respected, but at the same time some communal life should be available if it is wanted.

Old couples who are active may have their own bungalow or self-contained flat and live quite independently. More than a quarter of the housing built by local authorities now consists of one-bedroom homes, most of which are intended for elderly people. Two-storey blocks of flats have also proved useful, and in a few cases flats for old people have been included on the ground floor of multi-storey blocks. Bed-sitting room flatlets are sometimes available for the less active single person who would find a larger flat too difficult to care for. Such accommodation is deliberately mixed with that of younger people so that the elderly do not feel cut off from the rest of the community.

The government has recently taken an active interest in the interior design of such buildings. Design recommendations on housing standards for the elderly and other special groups are to be found in a series of manuals published by HMSO, and architects have shown much interest and ingenuity in adapting them for practical purposes. Large windows are recommended both for lighting and because for many old people this is an important means of contact with the outside world. The provision of adequate heating is recognised as a basic necessity, since it helps to alleviate many physical ailments like rheumatism and arthritis. Doors should have lever handles which are easier to open, and those on bathrooms and lavatories should lock but be openable from the outside. In the kitchen, cookers should be fitted with safety devices, shelves and work surfaces should be at an appropriate level, and cupboards should be built to a suitable depth for those who cannot reach far. Bathrooms are a particular source of danger; a handrail is needed to grip, a rubber mat in the bath should prevent slipping, and a seat across the bath helps those who find bending difficult. Hand-rails beside the lavatory are recommended, and non-slippery floors which are easy to clean.

Grouped flatlets with a resident warden provide appropriate accommodation for elderly people who can no longer manage in a bungalow or flat of their own. Tenants usually have their own room which they furnish themselves, but there are communal facilities such as sitting rooms, a laundry, storeroom and bedrooms for guests. Emergency call systems link the flatlets with the warden's quarters, so that a resident can obtain help at any time. Housing associations, like that of the Church Army and Abbeyfield, provide much of this accommodation, either by putting up new buildings or improving existing ones.

The elderly and handicapped eventually need a home where they are completely cared for, and yet are able to be mobile with a walking aid or wheelchair. The local authorities provide some homes of this kind, but many are private and some charge high fees. Much of the interior design already described is appropriate, though a recent government memorandum put forward some advanced ideas. It suggested that accommodation should be in bed-sitting rooms, each with its own lavatory and built-in cupboards. Lack of money prevents most local authorities from following this recommendation, but modern, purpose-built homes do now have a large number of single rooms, and provide sitting space in alcoves, halls and corridors as well as the usual communal rooms.

Most of the local authority homes provide good accommodation with residents paying a standard rate, or as much as they can afford. The drawback is that, in order to spread the overhead costs, they are often rather overcrowded. Privately run homes cannot meet these standards unless they charge very high fees, and some of them are not so well equipped. But they all have to reach a certain minimal standard and are inspected periodically.

In spite of these improvements in housing for the elderly, the handicapped and the homeless, a very high proportion of such people do not benefit and still live in very sub-standard accommodation. Nor are other aspects of housing much better. In cities like Cardiff and Newcastle, thousands of families are on the housing lists and an increasing number of homeless of all ages are sleeping rough. The lack of adequate housing is one of our greatest problems, and is the source of many other social evils.

6 The Family in a Community Setting

The area in which a family lives is just as important as the house in which it lives, for its members have to go to school, get to work and use many of the local facilities, such as hospitals, clinics, churches and places of amusement. They also need to form relationships with friends and neighbours if they are to lead happy and satisfying lives. Their way of life will vary depending on whether they live in a village in the country, in a suburb, or in the centre of a densely populated town; although in Britain modern methods of transport, like the motor car, mean that these differences are lessening.

Rural and Urban Areas
It is often forgotten that three out of every four people in the world still live in rural areas or in small towns dominated by rural interests, and in Asia and Africa as many as six out of seven people still live in such surroundings.

In Britain most people lived in rural areas until the industrial revolution. In 1790 there were twice as many people living in rural areas as town dwellers, but by 1840 the situation was reversed. Today only a very small proportion of the people live in the country.

Certain characteristics are common to most rural areas. For instance, conditions usually remain very much the same from one generation to another. Children replace parents, and are replaced by their children in turn, but the way of life carries on with little change from one decade to the next. The family is usually the centre of life with very close relationships between its members, often dictated by old traditions and customs. Most of the adults are involved in agriculture of some kind with a recognised type of handicraft, like spinning or wood carving, which they can do when the weather is bad or they are not required to work in the fields. Families may be scattered thinly over the countryside in farms, or they may live together in villages or small towns. This depends very much on the physical nature of the land and the sort of crops that are grown.

Changes come about, as they did in Britain in the late eighteenth and early nineteenth centuries when improved health and medical care led to a fall in infant mortality and a rise in the expectation of life. The increase in population that results from such a change upsets the balance of life in the country. The young can no longer find jobs in the rural areas and are lured to the towns by the prospects of higher wages and a more sophisticated way of life. It is mostly the children, the old and the less enterprising who are left behind in the rural areas to cope with the agricultural pursuits. So these have to be made less labour-consuming by the introduction of more modern mechanical methods.

As people move into the urban areas, these areas themselves begin to change. At first there is great overcrowding and the growth of cheap and poorly constructed homes. Gradually the urban area begins to develop a character of its own which is determined by the occupations of the people and the differences in wealth that industry and trade produce. These in their turn affect the way of life of the people living in the town.

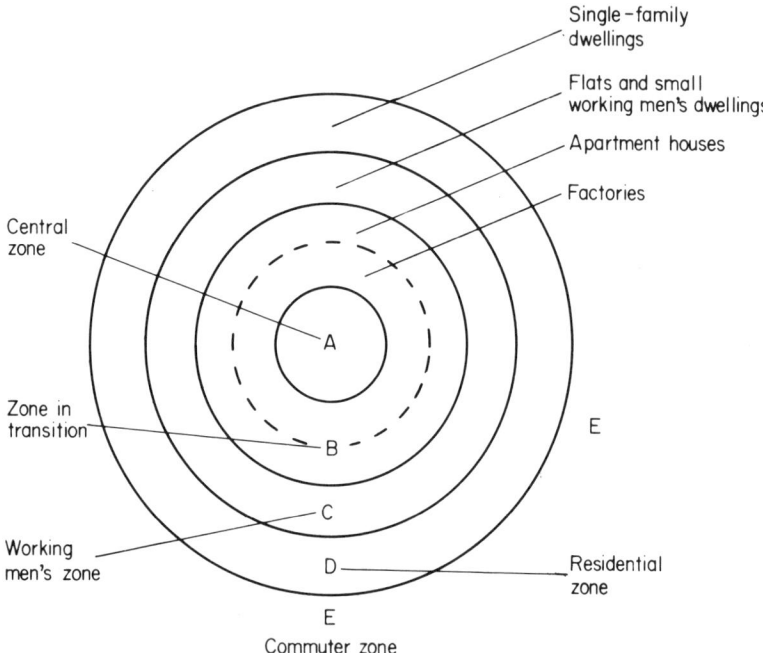

Figure 4 City structure: concentric zones

The Chicago school of sociologists in the mid-twenties studied the way this sort of gradual change took place. One of this group of sociologists, Ernest Burgess, produced a simple model of a city structure (see Figure 4) which he based on the concentric zone conception. This showed the pattern of city growth as a rough approximation of a bulls-eye. The central zone A was the business district with department stores, large restaurants, theatres and cinemas, the main offices and banks. Few permanent residents lived in this zone, but it catered for people who worked there by day and for tourists. Zone B was the area of transition where older private houses were being taken over for offices, light industry or conversion into cheap residential accommodation. It contained the immigrant and the 'twilight' areas of the city with their numerous drifters and homeless people. Zone C was the area where working people lived, where the houses were older, with few amenities, but a normal family life went on, with the usual social contacts. Zone D was the residential area, occupied mostly by middle class families, with newer and more spacious buildings and often called 'suburbia'. Zone E was the commuter or high-class residential zone, beyond the built-up area of the city, and probably up to a an hour's journey from the centre. Much of the commuters' zone would still be green fields and contain within it the original villages which were there before the area was built up.

This is an over-simplification of the development of most cities, but it does give some idea of a city structure. Homer Hoyt makes the development more realistic with his sector pattern, which shows how a city often expands in a wedge-like movement. Thus the upper class residential areas tend to be on one side of the city, rather than in a ring all round the centre. Industry tends to have its own area and to expand along the transport routes, and other smaller groups are fitted in, as can be seen in Figure 5.

A third pattern of city structure is the multiple nuclei pattern. This is often found where land is restricted, so that the city grows through the addition of segments or blocks in various places where there is vacant land (Figure 6).

These three theories on the ways in which cities may grow are models, and do not necessarily occur exactly as they are pictured. The development of many cities may be a combination of one or more of these processes. Cities built before mechanised transport are more likely to develop on the multiple nuclei pattern, but their more recent growth may be affected by bus routes and non-stop through traffic which leads to the sector form. In Britain the simple city centre on the lines of Burgess and Hoyt is more typical of smaller provincial cities like Hereford or Lincoln, which are old urban centres which had plenty of space to expand. London and the bigger concentrations of population have become an elaborate form of the multiple nuclei conception.

The period of greatest urbanisation in Britain was the nineteenth century, and this was to a very great extent due to industrialisation and the increase in town populations because of the chances of employment towns offered. This process continued throughout the

102 *Home, Family and Community*

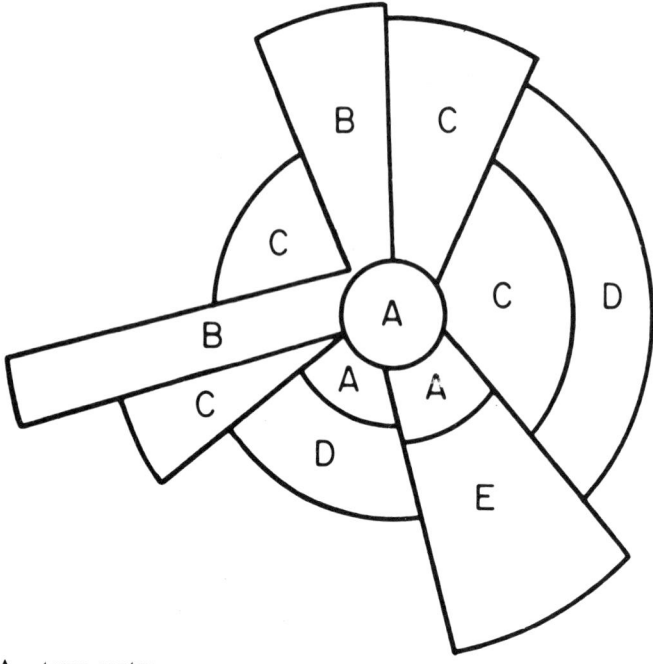

A   town centre

B   zone in transition which includes apartment houses and factories

C   working men's zone

D   residential zones

E   high class residential zone

Figure 5   City structure: sector pattern

century, so that big towns like London and Birmingham extended far beyond their existing administrative boundaries, building outer rings which linked up with neighbouring towns and absorbed them into single built-up areas. The term 'conurbation' began to be used in connection with such areas and became generally understood to mean a group of neighbouring towns which had grown by peripheral development into a single, continuous built-up area with common institutions, commercial life and social interests.

Because of this expansion of town areas and the merging of what were formerly isolated rustic parishes into the outer residential zones,

The Family in a Community Setting 103

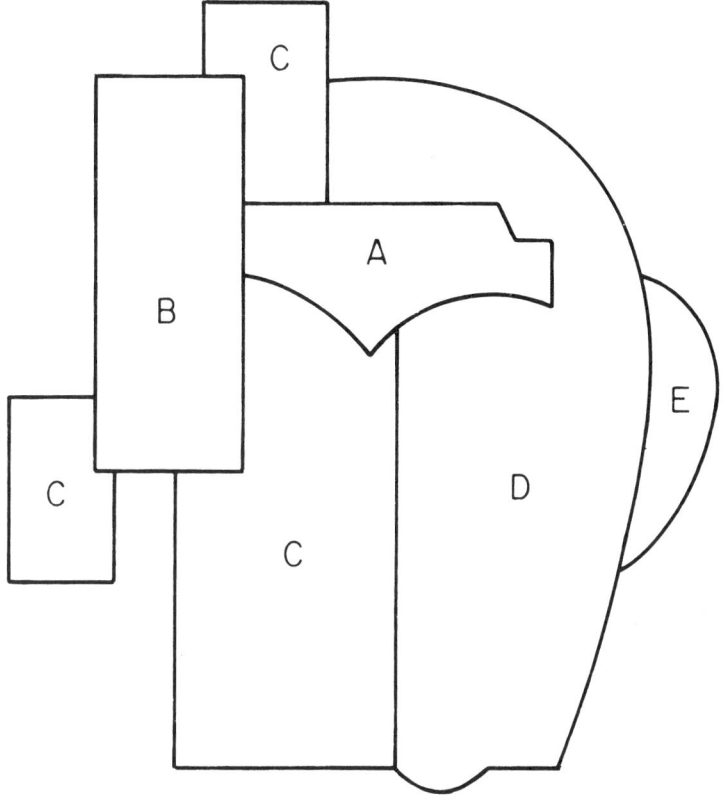

Figure 6   City structure: multiple nuclei pattern

the definition of a rural area in Britain is very difficult. It is by no means unusual to find a farm building in the middle of a large new housing estate, and to discover villages, like Blackheath in London, which in the past would have been completely cut off, becoming a dormitory suburb for an urban population. Therefore, in Britain the question is not so much whether an area is urban or rural, but to what extent it is a bit of both. It is often said that we have a rural-urban continuum, with the result that the inhabitants of the country and the villages, who are the rural people in the conventional sense, show a blend of urban as well as rural characteristics.

It is in the more remote areas of Wales and Cumbria that something close to purely rural life is found. A number of local community studies have been made, such as those of W. M. Williams on Gosforth, a village in Cumbria; Isabel Emmett and Alwyn Rees on

Birmingham: the photograph illustrates how the different business and residential areas have merged into a single conurbation

villages in Wales; and Ronald Blythe on Akenfield, in Suffolk. They describe in detail the characteristics of the area they cover.

For example, Alwyn Rees's study *Life in a Welsh Countryside* shows that most of the farmers lived on family farms and were engaged in the rearing of cattle. The family was the main social and economic unit with most of the work carried out by its members – father, mother, one or two married sons and perhaps a daughter as well. There was a rigid division of labour within the family, and outside help was only hired when the children were young or the parents growing old. Yet while family affairs were of primary importance, contact with neighbours was fairly regular, especially on important occasions such as the annual Eisteddfod.

Most such rural community studies, especially those in more remote areas, emphasise the continuing importance of kinship relationships, although, as W. M. Williams found in his study of a rural area in Devon, such relationships are becoming less important, largely on account of the greater mobility of rural people. But family connections still matter. Family members keep in far closer contact with one another than do the members of an urban family. If 'The Archers' are representative of rural families in Britain this is certainly the case.

Many families still have a deep attachment to the land. In many places the son takes over the farm from his father, who may then retire to the nearest market town. But in some areas farms change hands when the owners are no longer able to work them. This means that those coming into farming need to learn more about it, and they also have to be accepted by the other farmers in the area if they are to survive in times of difficulty. Young Farmers' Clubs help in this way, as do many of the other organisations in the market towns to which farmers usually belong.

Motor transport is rapidly reducing the distinction between rural areas and towns. Many villagers now work in the towns and make the journey of some five or ten miles by bus or car. Children who have passed primary level in education will go into the town to school, young people will find their entertainment there and housewives purchase much of what they need at the supermarket. The village is left with only the day-to-day shopping for staple foods, a limited amount of informal visiting and perhaps attendance at the parish church.

The situation is somewhat different in the commuter village. Here new people tend to outnumber the older inhabitants. They usually have larger incomes and would regard themselves as middle class. They live in cottages which have been restored and extended, or they build themselves modern houses on the sites of old dwellings. Their menfolk go 'up to town' to work, leaving the women to take an interest in what is going on in the village, such as the Women's Institute and the Mothers' Union. In many cases they provide the leadership for such organisations and manage the annual church fête. But although such people may seem well integrated into village life, this is often not the case. Affairs of any significance are frequently settled by the villagers themselves and there is an underlying feeling of resentment towards these newcomers.

Environmental Planning

Rural and urban areas both have their advantages and disadvantages. It was to try to bring together the advantages of both that Ebenezer Howard, in 1888, wrote *The Garden Cities of Tomorrow*. His concept was of a town built for both residence and industry. It should be small enough for the people in it to get to know one another reasonably well, and its houses should have gardens so that the inhabitants could both enjoy them and grow their own vegetables. A rural belt should surround the town with all the land in common ownership and held in trust for the community. This would prevent encroachment by other building and preserve the amenities of the town.

Though he did not actually advocate the planning of the environment, this is what his ideas led to. The Town and Country Planning Acts of 1909 and 1932 empowered local authorities to prepare planning schemes for almost any land, urban or rural, which was in the course of development. But this legislation was permissive rather than compulsory, so that many local authorities did not use their powers. It is only necessary to look at the 'ribbon development' along some of our country roads to realise this. Hence, during the Second World War, the Barlow Commission was asked to make a special study of the situation, and its report of 1940 became the basic document for housing and town planning for the next two decades.

The Town and Country Planning Act of 1947 at last imposed compulsory planning duties on all local authorities. They were given a fairly detailed control over the location, size and character of town and village development and over the sites of industrial estates. They were also to be concerned with the preservation of the countryside and the coast as places for members of the community to enjoy. From then on the government was required to maintain and enhance the amenities of the environment for all its citizens. This was continued by later acts and is now the duty of the recently formed Department of the Environment.

The new housing estates, built after the Second World War, followed a similar policy in that they envisaged the establishment of balanced and self-contained communities. But it took a while to learn how to do this. The first London County Council housing estate, built in the thirties at Dagenham, in Essex, failed to realise that something more than houses was needed. It provided no shops, churches, public houses, clinics or schools, because at this time little was known about the needs of a community. The inhabitants sometimes had to walk a mile or so before they could get any of these things. This was remedied in later housing estates where houses were built around the essential amenities.

The 'new towns' of Britain date from the New Towns Act of 1946 which extended the idea of Ebenezer Howard's 'garden city' to meet the needs of post-war Britain. These new towns were to be comprehensively planned communities where people not only lived but worked. They would come under the control of the Minister of Housing and Local Government who would appoint a development corporation to initiate the acquisition of land, carry out the building of houses, factories, schools, offices and shops, make provision for public services and administer the 'new town' until it was eventually handed over to the local authority. In actual practice, a Commission for the New Towns was set up in 1959 to supervise the final stages of development when the period of populating the town had been completed. This is what has happened with such towns as Crawley, Hatfield and Hemel Hempstead.

The way in which the development corporation functions is first to attract a number of diverse industrial and commercial companies to the town so that jobs are available for the people who are to be housed. Housing and other amenities like shops and schools can then be built, arrangements made for a few families to move in and a small community life started. This is then repeated until the town is fully grown. The usual requirement is that the head of the family should have a job in the 'new town'. But if he changes his job for something elsewhere, it does not necessarily mean that he has to move. The fact that the 'new town' is strategically placed at a distance of at least thirty miles from the conurbation which it relieves was intended to prevent this happening, though with improvements in transport quite a number of those living in the 'new towns' now have jobs somewhere else.

Over half a million people have moved into these towns during the past thirty years, most of them in the younger age groups with young children. This has meant that the age distribution of the population is unbalanced compared with that of the ordinary town. At first a 'new town' is composed almost entirely of young married people who require such things as schools and clinics. There are few middle-aged or older people and so little is done to provide the services that they need. As the years pass these young families reach middle age to find that the things they require are not always available. Similarly, the children as they grow up and marry are often unable to find anywhere to live in the 'new town' and have to go elsewhere. This accentuates the lack of balance in population.

108 *Home, Family and Community*

This new town concept of both living and working in a community has also been adapted to the extension of some of the larger existing towns. It was first tried in 1968 at Peterborough, which already had a population of 81,000 and was designated to take 70,000 more, mainly from London. The advantages of an already established town as a nucleus for such large-scale expansion are that public services, shopping centres and other facilities are already there and merely need expansion; that established industry has a chance to grow; and that it is possible to rebuild the run-down areas of the old town. All this is made easier by the existence of an experienced administration to work alongside the development corporation. On the other hand, a big drawback is that from a social point of view it is very difficult to integrate newcomers into an existing close-knit community.

The 'overspill' town is a somewhat smaller project and arises as a result of a voluntary agreement between the local authority in a big city and that of a country town willing to accept people in order to strengthen its economic position. Thetford in Norfolk is an example of this. Its industry was declining and there seemed little future for the town without the injection of families from elsewhere and the establishment of new industries. The way such a transfer takes place is for the city to publicise its scheme in the hope that firms looking for space will establish themselves in the country town. Families from the city and elsewhere are encouraged to move. This is a voluntary decision, but financial help is available from the city administration. Such schemes have proved popular, perhaps because they are on a smaller scale and people feel that they have moved of their own free will. Since the Town Development Act of 1952, which made schemes of this nature possible, more than sixty have been undertaken.

Problems of Urban Growth
The spread of the large towns and the development of conurbations in recent years have presented the community with two important groups of problems – those related to the environment and those connected with communications.

One of the most important and earliest of environmental problems is the collection of refuse and sewage disposal. Arrangements for this can vary widely. While in scattered rural districts the householder is often still responsible, in urban areas, and increasingly in rural areas too, refuse collection is financed out of local rates and carried out by the sanitary authority.

House, trade and street refuse, excreta (the waste products of the body) and waste water, all have to be disposed of. The householder is responsible for his own sanitary fittings and house drains and for the proper storage of his household refuse until it can be collected. For

This photograph, taken in Richmond, Surrey, during the prolonged dustmen's strike of 1977, illustrates the vital importance to the community of refuse collection and similar services

example, dustbins, which can be a serious nuisance, must have proper lids and be kept clean and free of flies.

Refuse, when collected, is usually burned, dumped or sorted for salvage. Where houses are connected with public sewers, these carry the sewage to the sewage works for treatment. But in many rural areas sewage is disposed of locally by various means such as cesspools or septic tanks, which have to be emptied at regular intervals since the untreated sludge cannot be used as a fertiliser without serious risk of infection.

Where sewage or factory effluent is discharged into rivers or the sea, pollution is often a serious matter, particularly along thickly populated coastlines. Similarly, the use of insecticides and sprays can harm plant and animal life. The Royal Commission on Environmental Pollution was set up in 1970 to deal with this problem. The outcome has been the giving of greater powers of control over pollution to the regional water authorities. But there still remains much to be done before the problem of pollution is dealt with adequately, as is evident when tankers inadvertently deposit their oil close to the shore.

Legislative control is exercised over a variety of environmental problems. The Litter Act, 1958, deals with those who leave rubbish around, while the Civil Amenities Act, 1967, provides powers for the removal of abandoned cars and other bulky rubbish. The Town and Country Planning Acts deal with such things as the display of advertisements or signs and posters which detract from the beauty of scenery, and with the siting of aerials and electricity wires, which must go underground when they would otherwise spoil the view. The Clean Air Act of 1956 empowers local authorities to declare 'smoke control zones' in which smokeless fuel has to be used for domestic purposes, and the amount of smoke from factory chimneys is regulated. Local authorities also have powers to take action against industrial and other forms of noise when it proves a nuisance to the public. It is obvious, therefore, that not only is concern over environmental problems growing, but that more attempts are being made to deal with them.

The most important communications problem is road traffic. About 90 per cent of the British people live or work in towns and with the high costs of public transport, many of them travel by car. In addition an increasing number of lorries and juggernauts use the main roads and take short cuts along the secondary ones. In a small and congested country like Britain, the towns were not designed to take so many large vehicles, while the winding and narrow country roads can cause accidents.

The Buchanan Report, *Traffic in Towns*, 1963, was the first major attempt to deal with this problem, and many later innovations stem from it. It is a comprehensive study of the impact on Britain of a large and rapid increase in traffic and it deals with both short-term and long-term policy. The primary purpose of the report was to keep through traffic away from the towns and in order to do this, a vast scheme of motorways is under construction. They by-pass the main towns, with feeder roads for traffic which needs to go into the towns.

Towns differ greatly and so each town has to decide how best to deal with its own traffic problems. This will depend on the capacity of the existing road system, the scale of investment which the town can undertake to ensure efficient traffic movement, and the value that the town places on such things as freedom from noise, fumes and danger in busy shopping areas.

Since the growth of traffic is outstripping the rate at which it can be coped with, certain short-term measures have to be taken. These include such things as one-way streets, clearways at times of heavy traffic and other devices to improve the flow of traffic. Parking controls such as meters and yellow lines are intended to keep cars out of congested areas, and off-street parking, particularly in multi-storey parks, caters for those who want to park for a longer time. Lorry routes and lorry parks, as well as controls on loading and unloading in built-up areas, help to deal with essential goods traffic.

Longer-term policy is concerned with the construction of new roads and the redesigning and widening of old ones. It has to balance the changes in the use of land or property against the advantages of improved traffic planning. In a built-up area like London this often involves the demolition of existing buildings and the dispersal of, for example, markets and industries to areas which are more easily approached by goods traffic. This has recently happened with the moving of the Covent Garden market out of Central London. In a country area the main concern is the relative value of land for agricultural use as against improved transport.

A recent development in the residential districts of towns has been to encourage traffic-free housing areas. The traditional street with access for traffic at the front and a pavement outside the door is now regarded as dangerous, too noisy and inconvenient. Instead it is proposed that there should be roads for motor vehicles only, a separate footpath system, and houses specially designed in groups with access for pedestrians and private cars. A self-contained path system should give an easy approach to every house and link houses with playgrounds, shops, schools and community life. It is impossible to do this in most existing housing areas, but it has been introduced with a degree of success, for instance in the 'new town' of Cumbernauld, near Glasgow.

It is fairly generally felt that communication problems include those of public as well as private transport. Public transport is used by commuters and those who cannot afford their own car, particularly the elderly. The authorities do little to help commuters because it is with them that their main profits lie, since they are a reasonably captive and regular market. But many local authorities are now providing free bus transport at certain times of day to pensioners, and British Rail have introduced special low fares for them. The basic problem is whether public transport should be a profit-making service or one which takes into account the welfare of the community.

The Community and its Development
The increase in urban growth has given rise to much loneliness and the feeling that nobody cares. This is the case not just in the inner city areas where people are constantly moving on. It is also true of the suburbs where families may take a long time to get to know their neighbours unless there is some drawing point like a school or a church which brings people together. Hence today there is much interest in community life, what it means and how it can be encouraged.

The meaning of 'community' is not easy to define, for the term can be used in a variety of ways; for example, there is the religious community where a group of like-minded people live together largely for the purpose of prayer. Or we may talk about the community from which the pupils at a school are drawn, and this usually means the local neighbourhood. In a community people are drawn together for some common purpose and, mainly for practical reasons, they live close to one another. Thus a community demands two things – a common locality and a common interest or purpose.

As far as living together is concerned, the members of a community may occupy a single residence such as a boarding school or a convent. More usually they live fairly close to one another in a village or the residential area of a town. Sometimes artificial units contain a community, such as a district or a parish. But whatever the boundaries of a community may be, they are not usually very strictly defined. Some members may live outside and still be members of the community. It is their common purpose which is the unifying factor.

This common interest or purpose cannot always be clearly indicated. If it is practical, like working together, it is fairly clear. But it may be some common attitude or belief which draws people of a similar outlook together and makes them feel at home with one another. It is this feeling of being 'at home' that binds a community together and so goes back to the earliest form of community which is the extended family.

A sense of community is usually fairly strong in a society which is relatively static. This used to be the case with villages and long established and traditional working class areas in this country. It is still the case in some of the developing countries which continue to follow their old traditions and folkways. But once changes begin, the old sense of oneness is lost. People begin to develop a feeling of 'anomie' or loneliness, of not belonging or not finding a niche in their surroundings. They find it more difficult to take any part in the decisions that are being made and they feel that things are being done for them rather than by them or with their consent.

This iş particularly the case as society becomes larger and more complex. The growing scale of central and local government, of industry and the social services, limit a person's opportunities for active participation and decision. He is part of a bureaucratic rather than a democratic society, and he exists as a unit or a number rather than a whole person. Yet deep down he wants to be regarded as a person in his own right, to have his needs satisfied as he would like, and to form closer social relationships with other people who have the same outlook. It is the purpose of community development to help in such a situation. It seeks to restore a sense of community when this has been lost, or to create it when it has never existed.

The original idea of community development arose from various self-help activities which Britain had used in her colonies in the tropics in the late nineteenth and early twentieth centuries. The intention was to help groups of people who had been moved from their homelands, or brought together indiscriminately, to gain some sense of living and working together as a community. Community development schemes became very popular in the less developed territories of Africa and Asia, both before and immediately after they had gained their independence. In the course of their operation, a great deal was learnt from these schemes about the application of such methods to different types of communities. Much of this information appears in the writings of T. R. Batten.

Although community development was originally associated with the developing countries, it was also applied to the relatively undeveloped areas of other parts of the world like southern Italy, Sicily and the Indian reserves in Canada and the United States. In places like this it was introduced as a means of helping to solve some of the problems of rural societies and backward communities which were rapidly coming into contact with modern ways of living. It is being used in Britain today to help forge social networks more closely and clearly in areas where there is little sense of community or contact between individuals.

A very similar situation to that of the developing countries a decade or so ago exists in Britain today. After the Second World War people did not necessarily return to their old jobs or their home surroundings, but were dispersed more widely over the country. In the same way, the movement of large numbers of people to the new towns and housing estates disrupted social relationships and social networks and led to various tensions and to the need to create new social contacts. The space in many of the 'twilight' or deprived areas of our cities is taken up by depressed minorities who may have fairly close family relationships but who are rarely socially integrated with the other people among whom they live. Many of these people feel lost and rootless and are unable to do much about it because they do not know what to do or may not even realise what they need.

The aim of community development is to help such people to know what they do need, or in more technical terms to realise their 'felt' needs. They may then feel able to do something about these needs, although they may require the support of other people in the local community with enough initiative to help them to put their ideas into practice. For this to happen there needs to be a good relationship between the people in the community and those who are helping. But the helpers' function is not to put forward their own ideas. They encourage the people themselves to 'feel' what they need and to initiate action to put these 'felt' needs into effect. The helpers are therefore 'enablers' who can be turned to in perplexity or doubt, but who do not take an active part in any decision making. This has to come from the people in the community itself.

Modern community development projects were first started on a small scale in this country by voluntary organisations which were trying to meet the needs of some difficult area. An example is that in Notting Dale, an area of north-west London where a large number of coloured immigrants lived. Race riots took place in the late fifties largely because immigrants felt that they were not accepted by the other people living in the area and were suffering discrimination. Ilys Booker, who had experience of community development work with Danilo Dolci in Sicily, led a team of workers to Notting Dale to try to help the inhabitants to come together as an integrated community. The purpose was to get both coloured and white people in the area to discover for themselves how to get to know one another more intimately and work amicably together in furthering the interests of both groups. They found that this could most easily be done through the schools and the various organisations for mothers and children. The ups and downs of this project can be followed in Mitton and Morrison's book, *A Community Project in Notting Dale*.

The government, in co-operation with local authorities, has recently sponsored community projects in certain areas where there are numbers of uprooted people and minority groups. These are usually the more deprived areas of the big cities to which immigrants and unhappy and unsuccessful people are attracted. The organisers of these projects encourage people to come together, and to put forward their own views on how to improve relationships within the area, and they help them to do this in practical ways.

The need for the development of a community spirit is not confined to the deprived urban areas. It is also required in the new housing estates and 'new towns' to which many people have moved. The National Council for Social Service has taken the matter up and fosters community centres in these new estates and towns. The community centre is intended to be a place where people who do not really know one another can come together for social, recreational and educational activities, either as members of groups following particular hobbies and pursuits, or on the basis of their common interests as local residents. In the 'new towns' these community centres are usually situated in the middle of the main residential area so that they can bring together the people in the surrounding neighbourhoods. On the new housing estates the community centre becomes the place where certain groups like the elderly, mothers with young children, and young people can meet together, get to know one another and follow their own particular interests.

Since the emphasis is on self-help, the community centre, which is available to all local residents, is usually managed by those who use it through a community association elected by the residents. Some of the larger ones have a paid warden who helps to bring together the older societies which may make use of the centre, and the newer community organisations. His job is to try to identify the needs of the locality, make the voluntary officers of the association aware of them, and in doing so create the conditions in which voluntary leaders may emerge. Thus he is concerned with the social needs of the whole area and seeks to create in it a sense of community with the community centre as a focus.

This idea of a community centre is being replaced in some places by community workers whose function is to make personal contact with the people themselves. Usually they are trained social workers, but with the community rather than the individual as their objective. They see families as forming part of the community and so try to help them to come together and organise their own activities for the different family members. Many of the 'new towns' and housing estates are employing such workers, and community work is rapidly becoming a very important part of the social work that is done there.

Neighbourhood and Neighbours
It is sometimes necessary to look at a smaller unit than the community – the neighbourhood – where social relations are likely to be face to face and therefore more intimate. A neighbourhood may be thought of in geographical terms as a distinct part of a city or town. It may be

defined by artificial barriers such as a road junction, a railway, river or a park, or even by the homogeneity of housing within the area. Thus a neighbourhood can be defined as a territorial group, the members of which meet on common terms within their own area for family occasions and for social contacts with friends who live nearby.

Sometimes it is easy to distinguish a neighbourhood. This is so with a suburb or small housing estate where there are a common type of housing and amenities, common interests among the inhabitants, and a reasonably similar pattern of social life. But in the inner areas of a town or city, there are usually very wide divergencies in the type of housing and the interests of the residents, so that they rarely know one another. It is only where there is some ethnic or racial homogeneity or some reason for similar people living close together that such an area can be described as a neighbourhood. An example would be a group of streets in Brixton where immigrants from the same overseas territory congregate.

Neighbourhoods tend to change in character, particularly in the inner city areas where people are constantly moving in or out. Thus wealthy families move out and their large houses may then be occupied by several families with smaller incomes, or rented out for businesses or shops. Warehouses, junk-yards and light manufacturing industry may appear. Deterioration will set in later. Homeless people will drift in and a high rate of delinquency will develop. Alcoholics, drug addicts and meths drinkers then find the area to their liking, and so an entirely different type of neighbourhood is created.

The character of the suburban neighbourhood may change less rapidly, for it is home to most families and so they will stay a reasonably long time. When they finally move their houses will continue to be used for residential purposes, and they will be replaced by people very similar to themselves. Unless there is some big change in the environment suburban neighbourhoods alter only imperceptibly as the property falls in value.

Since a neighbourhood is not only a locality but also an area where personal relationships count, the degree of neighbourliness matters to the people who live in it. A neighbourhood, whatever it is like, has certain functions to perform for its inhabitants and the extent to which it does so determines its degree of neighbourliness.

One of the most important of these functions is the socialisation of children. Unless the weather is bad, children are usually expected to play outside the home but reasonably close to it. They are influenced by the friends with whom they play and the sort of things they do. Parents can have some say in this by choosing the families with which their children associate. And so little cliques of families in which relationships are especially close may grow up in a neighbourhood.

But the children may be brought together by other means. Adventure playgrounds or similar amenities can do this and a church or club may have an overriding influence over them. Therefore the children in a neighbourhood may fraternise, while their parents remain aloof.

Help in time of crisis is another important function of a neighbourhood. Usually a family is ready to help neighbours in an immediate crisis, such as a serious accident or a death, even though it may not know them very well. But where continuous help is required, some neighbours are more forthcoming than others. A group of neighbours may sometimes co-operate to give help, and in doing so come to know one another much better. This can often lead to greater neighbourliness in the area.

A third function of a neighbourhood is social control. 'What the neighbours may say' can deter people from behaving in ways which do not conform to the customs of the neighbourhood. This function is strongest in the smaller and less mobile residential areas where people know one another well. But even in blocks of flats, where families do not know one another, such social control may still be exerted. Quarrelling or bouts of drunkenness can often be quelled by the attitude of neighbours.

Social class has some effect on the degree of neighbourliness. On the whole the lower income groups are far more neighbourly than those with more money. This may be a throwback to the time when more wealthy people had servants and so did not need the help of their neighbours. Various surveys which have been made of urban areas indicate this class link. Young and Willmott, in their studies of Woodford and Bethnal Green, both in east London, found that relationships are on a much more superficial and formal level in a middle class suburb like Woodford, than they are in Bethnal Green in the East End. In a working class area like this neighbours tend to come and go as they feel inclined and are ready for any sort of emergency. However, in a more deprived area, like Branch Street, Paddington, as Marie Paneth pointed out in her survey, the people are transitional, so there is only a very casual contact between families, and what neighbourliness does exist is more often than not kindness on the part of one individual to another. A typical slum, like Ship Street, Liverpool, described by Madeline Kerr, where people have usually lived for a long time, tends to be much more friendly. Here neighbours sharing a familiar background help one another more readily than do next-door neighbours who may be very dissimilar in outlook.

The Barlow Commission (see page 106) felt that there should be more neighbourliness between social groups, and suggested that houses in new residential areas should be varied in size and amenities so that they appealed to different income groups. But where this has been done, families in a minority in a neighbourhood have moved elsewhere to be among people of their own kind. The result has been that the area soon becomes, to all intents and purposes, a single class one. The same thing happens where middle class people buy up small property in a working class district. The area, after a time, develops the characteristics of a middle class suburb.

Some of the 'new towns' are therefore following a different type of neighbourhood principle. A neighbourhood unit is built to form a small grouping of houses and residents are chosen who are sufficiently alike in background to become closely involved with one another. The residential area, however, contains several different neighbourhood units so that different types of neighbours meet at the primary school, the shops and the welfare clinics, and this enables social contacts to be formed over a wider range. In private housing, the planning of cul-de-sacs can have much the same effect, although here the situation is brought about by the style of house and the purchase price.

Some of the surveys which have been done on urban neighbourhoods have been concerned with the problems of moving from a well-established neighbourhood to a new one. When a family from a working class area moves to a 'new town' or housing estate there is little choice as to neighbourhood or neighbours. They will usually know no one close at hand and this will not matter at first because they will need to concentrate on getting their new home in order. Housework can become an all-important task as the family feels a need to live up to its modern large front windows and its seemingly middle class amenities. But it may mean loneliness, especially for the wife who can find it difficult to get part-time work and who will not be able to see her relatives and friends very often. Integration into the community is usually slow, and a relationship of distant cordiality with neighbours lasts far longer than it would if the family had moved to an existing, well-established area.

When middle class people move it is often an indication of improved social status. The husband may have been promoted or obtained a better job and he needs to live among those of the same status. The family may therefore have to learn new ways of behaving in order to be accepted by a different social group. Social contacts are now more shallow and so it is not difficult to make new acquaintances. Certain forms of entertainment, like the drinks party, help. The family may also consciously alter its values and way of life to meet the demands of the new neighbourhood. But since such relationships are very much on the surface, it may take the family longer to feel fully assimilated than would be the case on a new housing estate.

Hemel Hempstead new town: shops and flats at Gadebridge neighbourhood centre

A special case, though one which is of great importance in some of our big cities, is the immigrant neighbourhood. When immigrants arrive their first aim is to find employment. Most of them are attracted to the 'twilight' areas of the large towns because here they are more likely to find a job. So they have to find accommodation near such an area. They will frequently live in large, overcrowded Victorian houses which have been divided into poorly adapted furnished rooms and are suffering from long-term neglect. More often than not the landlord is himself an immigrant who has usually had to borrow at very high rates to purchase the property. So he packs as many people as he possibly can into it, and to these are added any newcomers from the same country who may have nowhere else to live.

In such a neighbourhood these immigrant landlords come to be regarded as outcasts. The local inhabitants view them as undesirables who overcrowd and destroy good houses and lower the character of the neighbourhood. This means that the families are very much thrown in on themselves and are unable to make friends outside their own group. The only people who are likely to show signs of neighbourliness are those who have become deviants or left their own homes as a result of personal or family breakdown; and they may have very little to offer in the way of help or friendship.

Most immigrants are content to do their jobs and find amusement within their circle of friends from their own country. Problems of language and religion may make this essential. Their main contact with their neighbours is through the education of their children at the local primary school, and the school can help them to become a part of the neighbourhood. Some primary schools make a point of doing this, for example the Spring Grove School in Huddersfield, which is described by Burgin and Edson. Immigrant children here are not only given some language study; they learn about the British way of life. They are taken on visits to shops, factories, the public library, and the police and fire stations, so that they know about the local services which they or their parents may need, and get to know the people who provide them. Parents are encouraged to come to the school in the evenings and during the holidays to learn the language and customs of Britain and also to get to know the families of the other pupils. In this way they get an introduction to neighbours whom they might not otherwise meet.

It cannot be expected that the same sort of neighbourliness will arise quickly between British families and those from immigrant countries. This will only happen as they develop similar attitudes and outlooks, and in many cases this will take a long time. But they may learn to live together on a friendly basis and as time passes the newcomers may gradually find themselves assimilated into the affairs of the neighbourhood. Both sides can help with this. Immigrants need to take some responsibility for the community at large, and this has happened where they have joined the police force or been elected to the local council. But integration will not get very far unless they are accepted as neighbours by the British people. This is a situation which community workers are very much aware of, and one in which they should be able to help. But we also need more teachers who understand the problems of immigrant families, so that once the children attend school the family is linked with a British institution which is prepared to help it to become integrated into the community.

7 Social Services for the Family

In a pre-industrial society the family was expected to care for its casualties, and since the extended form of family structure was widely prevalent, this was usually possible. But there were always those who had no family ties, whose families were far away, or who had for one reason or another fallen out with their family. They were often helped by benevolent people, usually the wealthy, who regarded it as one of their responsibilities to do so. With industrialisation family members were separated, the younger ones moving to the towns, and the family was not always available to help in an emergency. The result was that those in need had to look increasingly to charity and eventually to the State to supply the sort of help they would previously have had from the family.

The Welfare State
Today we live in a welfare state, which means that the provision of most of the essential needs of the individual becomes the ultimate responsibility of the government. The welfare state was the outcome of a committee, chaired by William Beveridge, and set up in 1941 to look into the working of social insurance which had been in existence in a limited way since 1911. Beveridge's committee suggested that all members of the community should be included in the scheme on an equal basis, and that the benefits paid out in times of need should be sufficient to ensure that nobody's income fell below a prescribed minimum. To make this possible, supplementary benefit was to be made available to anyone not sufficiently covered by the insurance scheme who could prove his need.

Every adult now has to contribute to the social insurance scheme, though a distinction is made between those who are employees; those (the self-employed) who are working on their own or are employers; and the non-employed who are not receiving any monetary payment for work they may be doing, such as the daughter who stays at home to look after her elderly mother. In return for these regular (weekly) contributions, a person receives certain benefits when he falls into specified forms of need.

The main forms of benefit (specified by the Beveridge Report) are as follows: benefit for sickness, unemployment and retirement, as well as help at certain times of financial difficulty such as: maternity, when the mother can claim a grant and an allowance; widowhood, when an allowance, a widowed mother's allowance and an early pension are available; and on death, when a grant can be claimed by the nearest relative to help with the costs of the funeral. Since the rates of benefit rise from time to time in an attempt to keep up with rising prices, the best way to find out what the current rates are is to visit the local office of the Department of Health and Social Security and ask for the latest leaflets.

Until recently, the rate of contribution and of benefit was the same for everyone, provided he or she had paid the requisite number of contributions. But now there are income-related contributions and levels of benefit which provide a higher rate of benefit for those with incomes above a certain amount. This is a departure from the Beveridge principle of providing a minimum level of income for everyone, and is the beginning of an attempt to relate benefits to the standard of living of the particular family.

The position of the married woman in the insurance scheme has always proved difficult. Married women not at work did not have to join the scheme since they were covered by their husbands' contributions. Those at work could choose whether to pay the full amount or a reduced amount which only related to industrial injuries. In return, the benefit they could get was limited. But now all women are treated on the same basis as men, the only exception being those who have already opted out of the scheme.

Extra benefit can be claimed by a parent for dependent children, as well as for any other person a family may have to support. There is also a guardian's allowance for orphaned children, which is paid to anyone who takes such a child into his home; and there is a special child allowance for the children of divorced women.

National insurance numbers are allocated to everyone involved in the insurance scheme to ensure that their contributions are correctly recorded. Generally young people will have a national insurance number allocated to them before they reach school-leaving age. When a person starts a job he has to give his employer his national insurance number, and when changing a job he fills in a form showing this number which is passed on to his new employer.

If a person wants to claim supplementary benefit he has to go to the local office of the Department of Health and Social Security and give reasons why he needs it. Anyone can do this, although only those who fall within the prescribed categories of need will receive benefit.

Financial help from the State is supplemented by the personal services of social workers. These developed from the voluntary forms of help which grew up in the nineteenth century to deal with particular types of need, such as destitute children and homeless people. What usually happened was that first, some outstanding need, like the numerous ragged children to be seen in the streets, would attract attention; a group of people would then come together to help, and eventually the State would take over the work as part of its child care service. This led to a system of social services based on particular needs, such as destitution or delinquency, and when a family had a variety of needs it could be visited by a variety of social workers.

The importance of working with the family as a unit was discussed from time to time, but little came of it until the Seebohm Committee was appointed in 1968 with the specific purpose of securing an effective family service. The outcome was the Local Authority Social Services Act, 1970, which brought together the personal social services connected with the family and placed them under the control of the new social services department of the local authority.

These services include the work formerly done for children by the children's department, such as the care of underprivileged children; the home help service, for housewives who cannot cope with their domestic tasks; the welfare services of the local authority, particularly those for the handicapped and the elderly; the mental health social work services; local authority day nurseries; certain aspects of social work previously undertaken by the housing authorities; and a few other minor services. The social services departments of the local authority are now able to offer every family special services of a comprehensive nature which can be complemented by other relevant services, such as education, child guidance and probation.

The staffing of the social services has also been adapted to meet the needs of the family. Whereas in the past most social workers were trained for some specific purpose such as child care or hospital welfare, they now receive a general or generic training which fits them for all aspects of work with the family. To help these professionally trained workers, there are others with a practical or in-service training, as well as a large number of voluntary workers who offer their services free in their spare time, and usually help with the personal services, such as youth clubs, visiting old people and dealing with the handicapped.

The statutory social services are complemented by the voluntary ones. These consist of some of the old nineteenth-century charities, like the YMCA and the Girls' Friendly Society, as well as more modern organisations such as the Spastics Society. One of the purposes of such voluntary groups is to fill an immediate need and to hand the service over to the State later if it seems desirable. This has happened with many of the moral welfare associations which used to help unmarried mothers. Single mothers are now placed in the same category as all mothers. But sometimes the State likes to use voluntary societies on an agency basis and pay for their services. This usually happens when the service is one which applies to a relatively small group of people, such as the handicapped.

The Health Service is the social service which practically everyone in the community uses. It is both preventive and remedial. The basic aim of the service is the prevention of disease, as opposed to its cure, to be achieved, in co-operation with other services, through such improvements in the environment as better housing, a pure water supply, and the thorough removal of refuse and sewage, as well as through help and advice about nutrition, protection against infectious diseases by inoculation, and watching over the growth and development of the child so that any abnormality or defect can be dealt with promptly.

Only a part of preventive medicine falls within the scope of doctors. They advise, but much of their advice is left to others to carry out. Parents receive guidance from doctors or nurses, but the upbringing of their children is in their own hands. The local authorities deal with environmental health, and architects with such things as heating, lighting and ventilation of buildings. Many others are involved, including the statistician, whose figures on births and deaths and notification of infectious diseases help to indicate where further action is most urgently needed.

The health services of the nation were transformed by the National Health Service Act, 1946, into a largely free and generally available service. Its administration has recently been reorganised to make it more representative of local interests. It covers the services of the general practitioner, treatment in hospital and consultation with a specialist, as well as the many local authority health services such as the maternity and child welfare services.

The general practitioner service covers the medical attention given by doctors and dentists, which is normally free, though a basic charge is made for dentistry, spectacles, drugs and a few other minor items. Children under sixteen and young people still at school are exempt from some of these charges, as are expectant mothers and families with a very low income. The elderly can obtain free medicines and appliances and those who need frequent prescriptions can get a 'season ticket', whereby a single payment made in advance covers all the drugs which may be needed.

The establishment of health centres and community care is now replacing the doctor's surgery. At health centres a far wider range of services can be brought together, as well as consultant, dental and pharmaceutical services, and hospital out-patient services. This is helpful to both medical staff and patients, who do not have to visit different places at different times for treatment. Nursing staff, health visitors and social workers attached to such centres make it possible for a comprehensive service to be provided for the whole community, both at the centre and in people's homes.

Hospital services are also free, and hospitals are concerned not only to cure the patient but to rehabilitate him as soon as possible. This has now become an important function of the medical social worker, who is the chief link with the patient's family. Sudden emergencies are served by the free ambulance service, and fares can be claimed by a patient's relatives living at a distance if they cannot afford the cost of public transport.

Treatment for mental illness and subnormality are now part of the National Health Service. Patients can consult their family doctor and receive specialist advice at a hospital as they would for any other kind of illness and they can enter hospital without formalities. The Mental Health Act, 1959, combined with the use of tranquillising drugs, has made it possible for many people to receive treatment in their own homes. But this places an extra burden on the family, who may not fully understand the behaviour of the person concerned and may find it difficult to draw him or her into the ordinary life of the family. It was intended that the clinic, hospital and home should be brought together through the services of a social worker trained in psychiatry, but such workers are in very short supply. When a patient has been in hospital for some time there is often a need for half-way residential care between the hospital and the home. This usually has to be provided by some voluntary organisation like the Richmond Fellowship.

The disabled, whether blind, deaf, permanently handicapped or elderly, come within the care of the local authority. The Chronically Sick and Disabled Persons Act, 1970, has made it an obligation to provide not merely the minimal, but the best possible services that are needed, and this includes an attendance allowance for the severely disabled. The difficulty is to discover all the people who need such help, since registration with the local authority is only necessary in the case of the blind, who can claim an old age pension at the age of forty. Workers from the new social services departments visit and advise disabled persons in their homes. Social centres, recreational facilities and handicrafts are also available. Since such work does not require a great deal of skill, it is often undertaken by people with little training, such as the Community Service Volunteers who help the local authorities for a short time, receiving only their expenses and a small amount of pocket money.

The disabled can take advantage of both the rent and the rates rebate schemes if they have a low enough income. Wheelchairs and invalid vehicles are available for those who are unable to get around without them, including handicapped housewives, who may need a vehicle for such things as shopping. Most local authorities issue special car badges for parking, and more attention is being given to the problem of access to public buildings and places of entertainment for the handicapped. All kinds of other aids and appliances, such as adjustable handles fitted to everyday articles like combs, or hoists to lift and move the chairbound or bedridden, are also available and can be supplied to those who need them by voluntary organisations like the Red Cross Society.

Various domiciliary services are provided for the elderly to help them to stay in their own homes as long as possible. They share the home help service with the sick, the disabled and mothers of young children. A home chiropody service may be available, as well as a laundry service for the incontinent. Meals-on-wheels are frequently taken round by voluntary organisations like the WRVS, and for those over eighty, who are ineligible for the National Insurance pension, a special pension is provided.

In spite of the fact that the local authorities are obliged to provide residential accommodation for those with a low income, many elderly, disabled and chronically sick people are still found in the geriatric wards of the hospitals. The local authorities are doing their best to build homes and hostels for them, but with present-day cuts in expenditure, much is being left to the voluntary organisations. Societies like the Cheshire Foundation for the disabled and the Abbeyfield Society for the elderly do what they can to fill the gaps.

Special Provision for the Family
The basic family benefit used to be the provision of a family allowance, which was a cash payment drawn by the mother for the needs of the family as a whole, and was paid to families with more than one child. It was introduced in 1945, largely due to the efforts of Eleanor Rathbone who insisted that no social security scheme would attain its ends unless the needs of the larger family were taken into consideration. The Child Benefit scheme, which has replaced family allowances, enables the mother to draw benefit for each of her children, and it is intended that this should bring together tax allowances for children and family allowances in a new tax-free cash benefit for all children which will not involve families in any kind of means test.

For the mother and young child there are maternity and child welfare clinics in every local area to which the expectant mother is referred by her family doctor. They offer advice and mothercare classes before the birth, and, with the doctor, make arrangements for a midwife if the baby is to be born at home. Health visitors, who are state registered nurses trained for work with the family, encourage mothers to bring their infants to the child welfare clinic where they advise them on the care of the child up to the age of five. They also visit the home and give advice on many of the health and social problems which the family may encounter.

Liquid milk and national dried milk, as well as certain vitamins, are available at the clinic for all expectant mothers and young children. They are free to certain groups, including families with low incomes, or with several other children, and in special cases, such as handicapped children and children attending day nurseries or play-groups.

The child is not obliged to go to school until the age of five. But some mothers go out to work and others feel that their children need companionship, especially if they are 'only' children. Officially sponsored or approved day care in day nurseries and nursery schools, as well as registered private nurseries and childminders, are available. But given present financial strictures, there is little hope of a place in a local authority day nursery or nursery school. Most places are reserved for single-parent families and mothers who have to go out to work.

When the child goes to school he comes within the scope of a variety of social services. The school medical service developed as a way of improving the poor physique of school children in the early years of the century. Since the Education Act of 1944 it is the duty of the local authority to see that there are facilities for free medical attention for all school children. Some schools combine and share a school clinic, which is staffed by qualified nurses and has a doctor and a dentist available. Others make special arrangements with the local doctor and dentist.

A complementary service is the provision of school meals. This service dates back to the late nineteenth century, and the work of the Destitute Children's Dinner Society. The Education Act of 1944 made it a duty of local authorities to provide both meals and milk for children at school. School meals are provided at a subsidised price, with free meals for those children whose parents find it difficult to pay. School milk is now confined to children at primary school. The same Act makes it possible for grants to be paid towards the provision of school uniform and clothing for sports and physical training if parents cannot afford to buy them for their children.

Certain categories of handicapped children, including those who are blind or partially sighted, deaf or semi-deaf, epileptic, maladjusted or suffering from speech defects, may need special schooling. This can sometimes be given in the ordinary school, or it may mean sending the child to a special day or residential school. Several national organisations supplement what the State does in this area. The Invalid Children's Aid Association provides homes for chronically sick and maladjusted children, and cares especially for those who suffer from speech difficulties; the Shaftesbury Society is concerned largely with the physically handicapped; and the National Society for Mentally Handicapped Children helps the parents of mentally handicapped children.

The child guidance movement, which started in the United States in the 1920s, led to the provision of child guidance services in this country. They aim to help children who are unable to go to school because of emotional difficulties, or who seem unable to get on at school. There are now child guidance centres in most parts of the country, usually staffed by an educational psychologist, a social worker and a psychiatrist, and these centres are available to all children up to school leaving age.

One of the most difficult periods of life is leaving school and finding a suitable job. As a result of the Ince Report of 1945 the present youth employment service came into being, and now about half the school leavers between the ages of sixteen and eighteen get their first job through this service. A youth employment officer informs those still at school about openings in the locality. Arrangements are then made for individual interviews to which parents may come, and where possible jobs are discussed. The young person visits prospective employers, decides which job to take, and is contacted later by the youth employment officer to see if he is satisfied.

When the age of eighteen is reached the adult employment offices have to be used. They have undergone a great change since the days when they were known as employment exchanges. Their outward appearance and amenities have improved greatly and they offer a far greater variety of jobs. They now have special facilities for young workers, professional and executive staff and the disabled, as well as the beginnings of a vocational guidance service for adults which is being run experimentally in a few offices.

In spite of William Beveridge's suggestion that the State should help with the costs of marriage, this has not come about. Marriage and its problems are left entirely to voluntary efforts and since most marriages still take place in church, clergy and ministers of religion play an important part.

The National Marriage Guidance Council has also been taking an increasing part in the work of preparation for marriage and parenthood. Talks and discussions take place with young people in schools and clubs and with engaged and newly married couples in the homes of group leaders attached to the Council. The various aspects of married life which are discussed include home-making, sex, family planning and child-rearing, as well as financial matters such as budgeting.

There is still a need for an organisation which will help with the everyday problems of the ordinary family, since most agencies confine

130 *Home, Family and Community*

themselves to the exceptional or the deprived family. A few local authorities have set up family advice services for ordinary families as part of their child care duties, such as the family centre at Stevenage New Town where several different voluntary organisations have come together to provide advice and help. It is to be hoped that some of the newly organised social service departments will offer facilities for helping families with their personal problems.

Voluntary Organisations and Volunteers
Voluntary organisations have been concerned with family problems for a very long time. Probably the earliest was the Family Welfare Association, founded in London in 1869, which originally called itself the Charity Organisation Society because it was primarily concerned with preventing the overlapping of charities.

There are still a large number of voluntary organisations, ranging from comprehensive and well-known bodies like the Red Cross to small groups of local people who are willing to care for the family when a housewife needs help for a day or two during a short illness or an emergency. The Red Cross undertakes a very wide range of services, including welfare work in hospitals, such as trolley shops and canteens for out-patients, first aid and auxiliary nursing in the home, clubs and foot clinics for the disabled and elderly, holidays for handicapped children and adults, and escorting invalids when they need to travel.

Some voluntary organisations make far greater use of volunteers than others. For example the Samaritans, formed in 1953 to help those in despair or contemplating suicide, pay some of their professional counsellors, but the ordinary Samaritans are volunteers. Their main function is to offer a sustaining friendship to those who ask for help.

Many other forms of voluntary work go on in the community and include such things as clubs for young people, social entertainment for the elderly, recreational activities for the handicapped, feeding patients in hospitals and visiting the prisons. Every locality has a large number of groups which carry out some of these services, ranging from the purely local to branches of nationally organised movements, like Toc H, Rotary clubs and the British Legion. These three organisations all try to further a spirit of service and fellowship in the community. Toc H and the British Legion were inspired by wartime ideals of service, and Rotary, which consists of groups of professional people, has a similar purpose.

It has often been difficult for volunteers to find the sort of work they would like to do and equally for voluntary agencies to find enough voluntary staff. Therefore, in the last year or so, with the support of the local authorities, Volunteer Bureaux have been started in many areas to bring together potential volunteers and the openings for them. They act as a sort of labour exchange for voluntary work and have been most successful in increasing the numbers of volunteers working for the community.

The aim of social service has usually been to help others. An approach that has emerged recently is the self-help method, whereby people with similar needs share their experiences and give support and encouragement to one another. Cruse Clubs, which were started by Margaret Torrie in Richmond, Surrey, do this for widows, and Gingerbread groups bring single parents together. Weight-watching groups are a commercial example of the same principle. They bring together those who want to lose weight, but the cost of following their methods is rather high. Sometimes the self-help approach is used to organise a co-operative effort, as is the case with groups of young mothers who agree among themselves that one mother should look after the children while the others are free to go shopping, have their hair done or spend the day in town.

The National Council of Social Service was formed at the end of the First World War to bring together this rather heterogeneous range of voluntary organisations. Since then the Council has done much to start and support the work of volunteers. One of its most important contributions has been the Citizens Advice Bureaux which have been set up all over the country to answer the questions of the ordinary citizen and deal with many of his difficulties. These include such things as family and personal problems, housing difficulties and, with the fall in the value of money, how to meet outstanding debts.

Most towns and cities have local social service councils whose main purpose is to co-ordinate the social services in the area. The intention is that they should be information centres for the different statutory and voluntary groups in the district and provide for joint consultation between them. They are usually the co-ordinating centre for much of the voluntary work that is done for families in the area, and are often the means by which new projects can be discussed and tried out.

The volunteers who undertake these various services are frequently parents or older children, and especially the mother whose children are growing up. Young people, too, are taking a far greater interest in community services than they did in the past. Organisations like Voluntary Service Overseas and the American Peace Corps set the example after the Second World War, and now the attention of many young people is focused on helping in their own country. Older pupils at the local school may visit the elderly, do their shopping or gardening or any other job which they cannot do for themselves. Student Community Action, organised by the National Union of Students, does such things as repairing and decorating houses in poor areas, and helps other young people through its student-run advice and information centres. It also undertakes research into social problems such as the extent of hypothermia, or death from cold, among the elderly, and what steps should be taken to prevent it.

Much social service is given by the churches and they are well placed for this, as they usually cover a definite area and can call on a body of volunteers to help. The Anglican church, and some others, do occasionally employ professional social workers, but by far the greater amount of such work is of a neighbourly or community nature. For example, in one Oxford parish a 'fish' scheme was started, so called because a fish sign is placed in the window by anyone in need of help. The parish has a rota of people willing to respond to such calls, which may involve doing shopping, running errands, giving lifts to hospital or to the town hall, baby-minding while the mother is out, or helping with young children if she is not well. Local members of a church may start special kinds of work, such as a home for elderly people or a fellowship to make friends with patients in the local mental hospital.

Much of the local voluntary community service is fostered by women's organisations like the Women's Royal Voluntary Service, the National Council of Women, and the Women's Institutes. Such organisations have a twofold purpose – acting as pressure groups in matters which specifically concern the welfare of families, and organising special areas of community social work which may have been overlooked by others. They may also combine these with cultural and educational activities.

The WRVS concentrates on the social service aspect. Started during the Second World War by the government to help with war conditions, it is now called on by the police or local authorities to deal with emergencies such as accidents, floods, fire or the arrival of refugees. But its main function is to provide the services of a good neighbour, such as taking round meals-on-wheels to the housebound, organising residential and day clubs for the elderly, serving in canteens, undertaking spare-a-mile transport for the elderly and disabled, and collecting used clothing from the public to be given to those in need.

The National Council of Women, which was originally concerned with the legal and voting rights of women, is now more of a pressure group. It was deeply involved in the campaign for cervical smears, has taken a leading part in the reform of the law on abortion, and is to the forefront in the publicity given to the problem of battered wives.

Women's Institutes also go back to the late nineteenth century, although they became prominent in the First World War in their work with the Ministry of Food. Lady Denman, who directed this work, became the first president and adapted the work of the organisation to peacetime. At the village level, the local Women's Institute now provides opportunities for contacts between the different social groups and for newcomers to be brought into village life. It is also a means of developing household skills and other homecrafts, and those who are interested can go to Denman College for more specialised courses. At the national level the organisation brings matters of concern to women to the notice of the government.

The Mothers' Union, though basically an Anglican organisation, is somewhat similar in its purpose to these three women's organisations. Its chief concern is the family – both family relationships and the care and wellbeing of the children. Although its special emphasis is on the sanctity of marriage, since the recent review of its work (1977) it has admitted divorced and separated people to its membership.

A rather different form of voluntary service is that provided by the local magistrate or Justice of the Peace. This is one of the oldest forms of service and used to be confined to the leading male citizens in an area. Now any suitable adult may be chosen to undertake it, and the choice depends on the character of the person concerned and his or her involvement in local affairs. Government policy today is to encourage younger people and those from the lower income groups to be put forward for selection. This is partly because the main function of the JP is to administer justice in the magistrates' courts, and many of those who come before the courts are from the younger age group. Housewives are frequently used for work in the juvenile and domestic courts, and they often combine this with other forms of local voluntary service with the result that they are particularly knowledgeable about the community in which they live.

The fullest involvement in community life comes through election to the local council. Ever since such councils came into being at the end of the nineteenth century, men and women have been able to put themselves up for election and, if chosen, to participate in the policy making of the local council. This means dealing with local matters such as the amenities of the area and the welfare of the people in it. It offers a unique opportunity to bring about improvements in community life, and there is always a specific committee on which the councillor can sit if he or she is deeply interested in some matter. Housewives with older children often stand for election and are able to make the sort of contribution which would be outside the range of competence of the other members of the council.

Socially Deprived Families
In spite of the fact that the welfare state should ensure that everyone reaches a reasonable level of income, some people fail to do so. There

are various reasons for this. A large number of such people are earning very low wages against which they have heavy expenses that the State is not empowered to meet. Others have small social security benefits and are unwilling to claim supplementary benefit, which is intended to bring their incomes up to the average level of those on social security. For quite a number the problem is an inability to use properly the resources that the social services can provide. In the present economic crisis, unemployment and the difficulty of finding a comparable job locally account for many more cases.

Families where this is the situation are termed 'deprived' because they are without access to the comforts and self-respect which other members of the community enjoy. The difficulty is that once income deprivation occurs it is likely to lead to other kinds of deprivation. The family may have to move to less adequate accommodation and this means housing deprivation. The children may be affected through lack of care and of some of the material things they are used to. They often do badly at school, leave early and enter unsuitable employment. In fact it is quite usual to talk about the 'cycle of deprivation', meaning by this that families which are deprived tend to have children who will form families which are also deprived. Thus deprived families reproduce corresponding failings and inadequacies from one generation to the next.

The State does its best to help families suffering income deprivation. The majority of such families come within the scope of the family income supplement which is payable to families whose gross income is less than the amount prescribed by the government. Such families are also entitled to free medical prescriptions, free dental treatment, free school meals, various vitamin foods and milk as well as a few other things.

Quite a number of such families are single-parent, either because the mother did not marry, or because the husband is no longer there for some reason and has left her without adequate financial provision. Some may be widows with young children and others may have a husband who is in prison for a long spell. Voluntary organisations help many of them. One of these is Gingerbread, which now has groups throughout the country giving advice on every aspect of the situation, from maintenance to registered child-minding while the mother goes out to work.

Though the immediate cause of deprivation is inadequate income, especially when this has to keep a large family, a basic cause may be an inadequate personality in one or both parents. This may be because they are of low intelligence, or have been in and out of a mental hospital. Such things can seriously disrupt family life, and make a normal existence impossible. Families affected in this way are by no means confined to the lower income groups. They are to be found in suburban areas as well as on council estates. But suburban families are more likely to have relatives who are in a position to help, and so they do not come to the public notice so frequently.

Deprived families seem to gather in the more run-down areas of our cities, where they can find cheap accommodation and follow their own disorganised way of life, untroubled by their neighbours. Small pockets of such families are often found living in a cul-de-sac or a row of nineteenth-century workmen's cottages, where they live as they please and are ignored by the rest of the inhabitants.

The social services are responsible for helping such families, but because of the multiplicity of their problems few social workers have adequate time to spend on them. They are frequently referred to the Family Service Units which are able to give them more time and intensive care. These units originated during the Second World War to help families made homeless by bombing, and when the war ended they turned their attention to problem families.

The special method adopted by the social worker dealing with this area is to identify with the family, showing understanding and concern so that members of the family come to trust him and use his help to become more independent and regain some self-respect. Help is given in a practical way – cleaning and decorating the home, providing clothes and furniture, helping the mother to cook appetising meals and care properly for the children. This can take months, or even years, and only about one family in ten achieves any real change in its mode of life. But at least some families are kept together and a few manage to reach a minimum standard of family management.

This sort of help is of little use where the mother is inadequate or unequal to her everyday tasks because of poor health or too many children. For such families there are a few rehabilitation centres where they can go to learn how to cope. These were pioneered by voluntary organisations, but are now run in co-operation with some of the local authorities. They offer residential care for mothers with their children, and sometimes fathers, who are expected to obtain a job locally.

The family is usually given a small flat for a period of several months so that the mother can start afresh and have a chance to regain her health. She is taught to budget, cook, keep house and manage her own life and that of her children. During the day the young children are cared for in the nursery so that the mother can concentrate on the other things she has to learn, and can also be taught something about child care. The testing time is when the family returns to its own home, for what has been learnt has to be applied in very different conditions and in a much more complex situation.

All children who are deprived of a proper home life are not necessarily the children of deprived families. They may be children with unsatisfactory home conditions, such as a mother who lives with various men, or constant quarrelling in the home. They may be children who are orphaned and have no relatives or friends who are willing to take them in. Their parents may have deserted them, or maybe are in prison or a mental hospital for a long time. Such children come into the 'care' of the local social services department and may spend a considerable part of their childhood in care. On the other hand, most of the children who are helped in this way are only in care for a few weeks or so, usually because the mother is in hospital or is temporarily unable to look after them for some other reason.

A certain number of children who come into care are sent by the courts, because it is thought that their homes are unsuitable. Sometimes parents ask for them to be taken into care because they are unmanageable. The Children Act 1975, gives local authorities a much wider responsibility for such children, leaving it to social workers, parents, the schools and the police to decide how best they should be cared for and treated.

When possible, these children are placed with foster parents, who are recruited from all sections of the community, paid an allowance sufficient to cover the maintenance of the child, and expected to give him or her the same care as they would their own child. They usually have children of their own, and so the foster child has a chance to experience normal family life.

A number of problems arise with fostering. The law says that foster parents have to allow the natural parents to visit the child, and if the parents are at any time thought able to look after the child, he or she has to be returned. If the child has been with his foster parents for a long time, this can cause distress both to the child and to the foster parents. Several cases of this nature have arisen recently, and this right is being questioned. On the other hand a child who is fostered may pass through the hands of several foster parents and never have time to feel really at home. One or two adults who were fostered in childhood and have written about the experience claim they would have preferred to go to a residential home.

All children's homes, since the Children's and Young Persons' Act 1969, are known as 'community homes', although they still provide a range of specialised forms of care to suit the needs of different types of children. Thus some are geared to the difficult child and others are short-stay homes for a child whose mother or father may be unable to look after him for a few weeks. A considerable number of the children are of mixed race, for it is much more difficult to find foster homes for coloured children. Many of the community homes are run by voluntary organisations, like Dr Barnardo's and the Children's Society. Nowadays they are small in size, usually mixing the sexes and age groups, so that the conditions of family life are reproduced as far as possible. In fact in an experiment by one local authority, a house mother and father were given a large house by the council with a 'ready-made' family from a baby to teenagers.

The alternative to fostering or residential care for a deprived child is adoption. This is a legal arrangement whereby the adoptive child belongs to his adoptive parents and has virtually the same rights as if he had been born to them. Legal provisions for adoption were first made in 1926, though they were modified by the Children Act of 1975 which followed the Lane Committee Report. This Act allows only local authorities and officially approved societies to arrange adoption. The Adoption Act, 1976, consolidates the previous provisions, bringing the position of the adopted child onto almost the same footing as the child born to his adoptive parents.

Adoptive parents are very carefully selected by social workers, and there is a trial period before the adoption is legally finalised. Many of the children available for adoption are infants, often those of single mothers who are unable to care for them. This may happen if the mother is still at school, or feels that she cannot cope with a job and looking after the child on her own. Some mothers, in later years, very much regret giving up their child in this way, particularly as they have not been told who the adoptive parents are. Similarly adopted children often want to know the names of their parents and to meet them as they grow older. It has therefore been made possible for adopted children, under certain circumstances, to meet their natural parents, if both parties want this, when the children are grown up.

Deprivation due to personality traits can often be the result of addiction to drink or to drugs on the part of the parents or young people. In spite of the publicity that is given to drug addiction, alcoholism is far more widespread. Very generally, there are more than 300 alcoholics to every drug addict in Britain, and deaths from alcohol far outnumber those caused by the misuse of drugs. But drugs get more publicity because of the sordid conditions in which many addicts live, and the disastrous effects which drugs can have.

Alcoholism is on the increase among young people, partly because they have more money to spend, and also because of the uncertainties of life today. It is also reaching the younger age groups. Children of twelve, thirteen and fourteen often look so grown up and sophisticated that it is difficult for the publican to challenge them.

Until recently alcoholism was regarded as a problem of middle age. It still is, though whereas ten years ago the ratio of male to female alcoholics was eight to one, it is now three to one. Among the reasons for this are domestic stress, especially the isolation and loneliness experienced by many women with young children, and also the fact that it is now much easier for women to buy drink, for example in the supermarket while out shopping.

The effect of alcoholism in one parent can be very disruptive to family life. If the father is the alcoholic, financial strain will inevitably result. The mother may have to keep the home going with her own earnings, and at the same time suffer the barely concealed comments of neighbours and friends, in addition to the effects which all this can have on the children. If the mother is the alcoholic, the home will be neglected and the children will be left to their own devices.

Treatment is difficult to obtain, for few alcoholics are willing to admit the truth, and few hospitals specialise in such treatment. Many family doctors are not sufficiently interested or informed to do much about it. Those who want to give up drinking often turn to Alcoholics Anonymous, which was one of the first self-help organisations. It is run by alcoholics, who meet to support one another in the difficult task of giving up drinking.

Drug addiction is largely a young people's problem, although parents and older people can be affected, especially if they have been prescribed drugs as a medicine and become addicted to them. Many people in middle age rely on drugs to help them in a crisis or period of depression.

Young people often take drugs because they are highly effective in overcoming shyness or the sense of being the 'odd man out' at a party. The danger lies in the 'it won't happen to me' attitude. This leads to an increasing intake or a change to a stronger drug. But drug-taking usually becomes a habit because there is a personality weakness which is laid open by some crisis at the same time as the drug is available. Others who become addicted are the footloose and jobless young in the inner city areas who have nowhere to live and nothing to do all day. An organisation which seems to be having some success in helping such young people is Release, a voluntary organisation run by young people.

Cigarette smoking can also become an addiction, especially if it reaches chain-smoking proportions. This happens with many very young adolescents, some of whom smoke an incredible number of cigarettes in a day. They reach the stage where they cannot do without smoking and will go to any lengths to get hold of cigarettes.

Community care is an important way of dealing with addiction, whether to drugs or alcohol. The willing acceptance by others of a state which a person is basically ashamed of, and which he feels cuts him off from friends and relatives, can do a great deal to help him throw off the addiction. A close-knit and loving community, such as the

Cyrenians, offer surroundings which may make an addict feel he is able to stand on his own feet and lead a normal life again. Yet there are many addicts for whom there seems to be no way out, and for whom society appears to have nothing to offer.

The Development of a Sense of Responsibility
Although the welfare state has provided much-needed social services for the community, it has led to a certain amount of irresponsibility on the part of some of those who receive these services. They have come to think that they receive them as a right, while some go even further and think that it is quite legitimate to take as much from the State as they possibly can, by fair means or foul.

It is quite true that the benefits received as a result of social insurance have been partly paid for by the recipient through his weekly contribution. But the State has also contributed, sometimes quite a large amount, and in the case of supplementary and child benefits and other non-contributory benefits, all the money has been provided by the Treasury. Even in the National Health Service, only about 10 per cent of the cost comes from the social security contributions of individuals.

Reports are constantly appearing in the newspapers of cases of abuse of the statutory social services. Unemployment benefit is claimed when a person has made little attempt to find work; or highly relevant facts are withheld when supplementary benefit is asked for. It is difficult to estimate the extent of such abuse, although its prevalence is connected with a sense of injustice on the part of people who feel that the State has cheated them in so many ways that they have a right to get their own back.

To some extent this has been due to a failure on the part of the welfare state to consider its consumers. The State has adopted a domineering attitude and little attention has been given to complaints from those who make use of the services. This has recently received some attention in the health service, where patients have been given definite channels through which they can complain if they are not satisfied; and for some time now the Ombudsman has dealt with complaints in this area.

As well as this, voluntary societies have been formed to monitor particular services. Societies like the National Association for the Welfare of Children in hospitals have done much to improve conditions in children's wards and to make it possible for the mother to stay with her child if he is unhappy without her. At the local level, groups of people have pressed for such things as a small kitchen to be made available in an old people's home or club so that the residents or members can cook themselves simple snacks or make a cup of tea.

There are a number of welfare services which the local authority can undertake at its own discretion. These include such things as arranging recuperative holidays for people who have been ill, or running a laundry service for the incontinent. The local community needs to be aware of this, and to exercise enough pressure to get such services started.

Similarly, information about the local social services may not be readily available. Local authorities need to be persuaded to display information about their activities in the post office or the public library. This applies in particular to such things as supplementary benefit and the various welfare concessions which can be obtained by those who claim the benefit.

There may be some services which are not exactly what the community wants, and quite often they are services which absorb a large amount of public money. This can be said of many of the residential homes for the sick and elderly, whose inmates would prefer to live in their own homes or with their family, if only more help could be given to them there. The attendance allowance, which is paid to the severely disabled who live at home, has gone some way towards remedying this. But the difficulty is to find the sort of help that is needed.

Situations like these can be rectified if those who are aware of them come together and publicise them. Sometimes this can be done through existing pressure groups like the National Council of Women. But more often it requires a pressure group set up specifically for the purpose. This is what Peter Townsend found, when he formed the Child Poverty Action Group to draw attention to the needs of the many children who were deprived of a proper home life, and of whom most people in the community were almost entirely unaware. As a result far more attention has been given to the needs of these children, and there have been some changes in the existing legislation.

A sense of responsibility towards the community can involve more than seeing that the social services in the area are being carried out adequately, and that those who receive them are fully considered. It can also mean taking some active part in helping others who may be in need. There is always a place for the volunteer in the many voluntary organisations which exist in an area, and in some of the statutory ones.

8 Homes of the Future

It is always difficult to try to look into the future, in a period of rapid social change such as we are experiencing today. One of the greatest failings of the amateur prophet is giving undue weight to the immediate past, so that his predictions become little more than naive projections of recent events onto the far distant future. It is better to look closely at the basic long-term changes which are taking place, and consider their possible future effects.

Thinking ahead in terms of the home does not merely mean considering what structural changes may take place; what improvements in labour-saving equipment may occur; what changes in methods of cooking and heating may be appropriate; or what new ideas of home management may develop. It involves going deeper than this, seeing what lies behind these changes and so looking first at the trends in world and national conditions. It is necessary to see how these may influence the home, and the family's way of life.

Since the Second World War there has been a great increase in world population, much of it concentrated in the developing countries, particularly in Asia and Africa. But this has not led to a redistribution of commodities and resources to meet the needs of the people concerned. Instead, there has been competition for the limited supply of available resources, and some countries, usually those countries which are less developed and are sometimes referred to as 'Third World' countries, have been left behind.

Not only does the Third World require more foodstuffs and raw materials; the Western world has also greatly increased its demand for them. This is because of the increase in wealth and its more even distribution. To meet this demand there needs to be a great increase in the gross product of most countries, especially those which concentrate on agricultural products and raw materials.

Since this is unlikely to take place on any scale in the next few decades, the Western world will have to face a situation in which some of the more familiar but costly foods, like meat, will have to be replaced to some extent by synthetic products. This could, in time, lead to quite considerable changes in the diet of people in the Western world.

To try to defer such a situation in Europe, the European Economic Community – the EEC – came into being in 1958 (although Britain did not become a full member until 1973). The purpose of the EEC is primarily to bring about closer co-operation between its member nations, both economically and politically, so that all may work together more efficiently not only to produce a greater gross product, but to do so more cheaply and to be able to distribute more evenly the products that are required by all.

At the moment the EEC is engaged in laying down a set of common policies for its members, relating to agriculture, transport, social welfare and commercial undertakings. It is hoped that in this way the member nations will be better able to co-operate with one another and with other countries on such things as the supply of foodstuffs, energy requirements, the production and movement of goods and the welfare of people. An indirect result should be to induce further co-operation between Europe and the rest of the world.

The immediate effect of Britain's joining the EEC on the British housewife has been the introduction of the new decimal currency, which after its initial difficulties is now accepted by most people, except perhaps the elderly who may still find themselves converting what they buy into pounds, shillings and pence. This is being followed by the metrification of both weights and measures, which will place all the countries in the EEC on a common basis. Troublesome as such changes may be when they are first introduced, they do enable trading to be done more easily, and so cut costs.

Housewives are also very much aware of the rise in prices of practically all foodstuffs and household foods. This is partly due to inflation, but it is also connected with the equalising of prices within the EEC countries. The long-term effect of the latter policy should be that a greater variety of goods will be available on the shelves of the supermarkets. The common agricultural policy should mean fewer shortages and so more constant prices for basic commodities like bread and milk. The wider movement of capital and labour could lead to more inventions and innovations in products for the home, as well as lowering their costs. This is already illustrated by an investigation which took place into the production of domestic electrical appliances in Germany, France, Italy and Belgium in the late sixties, which showed that an increase in the production of these goods was accompanied by an appreciable fall in the average price of washing machines, refrigerators and cookers throughout the Community.

Since the 1960s there has been a mounting concern about man's impact upon the natural environment. Many fear that continuous economic growth, coupled with a wasteful use of both energy and raw materials, will so increase both the demand for resources from the environment and the output of large quantities of waste, that global disaster could follow. Thus pollution and depletion of resources become twin concerns which have to be considered together.

Various suggestions and experiments have been made to deal with

Homes of the Future   143

waste and avoid pollution, including the recycling of materials. This means converting waste products into useful materials which can be used again in the process of production. The difficulty in doing this is cost. So far, recycling in most cases is not financially viable. There is a great deal of waste produced in the home which has to be collected and disposed of and which could, if the costs of recycling were not so high, be used again. Examples are containers, paper and even used water which could be cleansed and re-supplied.

The present concern over fuel shortages is another aspect of the problem of man's impact on the environment. The oil crisis, which was precipitated by OPEC (the Organisation of Petroleum Exporting Countries) in the third quarter of 1975, drew attention to the heavy dependence of modern technology on constantly increasing and reasonably cheap supplies of energy. Previously coal had supplied much of this, either in its natural form or by conversion into gas or electricity. With changes in relative costs, oil proved a cheaper substitute. Even if OPEC's power to push up oil prices lessens in time, the problem of finding increasing supplies of energy to meet all the needs of modern industry, transport and heating will still remain.

Since other existing types of energy seem unlikely to be able to expand sufficiently quickly to fill the immediate gap, we are faced with a long-term increase in the cost of energy relative to other goods and services. This could mean dearer prices all round, which would hit the home partly in higher prices for goods and services, but also in the cost of heating and cooking.

There is therefore a need to develop alternative new sources of energy. This could involve non-fossil sources which are not subject to such restricted supply. They include geothermal heat which is recovered from the depths of the earth, hydro or electric power, and tides and winds, some of which have been used for some time on a small scale in different parts of the world.

A much more likely major source of energy in the future is the sun, which already provides part of the energy needs for some agricultural uses. Solar energy has many advantages, including its world-wide distribution, its safeness, its freedom from significant changes in environment and its enormous quantities. It has already been tapped in various parts of the world in the form of house heat-collectors which provide energy for both heating and cooking, and there appears to be considerable scope for expanding this use of solar energy. Its use to generate electricity on a large scale is likely to be more difficult and costly since it means devoting large areas of land to tapping the energy and overcoming the problems of cloud cover.

The building research section of the Department of the Environment in Britain is studying various ways of conserving energy in the home. One of these is the solar house which would use energy from the sun. A second reclaims energy from the air ventilation system and waste hot water; and a third – a heat pump house – extracts heat from the outside atmosphere. If any of these three types of house could be constructed at a sufficiently low cost, and without altering the life style of the people living in them too much, they could go some way towards reducing the inevitable rise in the cost of heating and cooking in the home of the future.

Apart from energy, other costs are likely to increase in Britain in the future if the present inflationary trends continue, and if there is an increasing demand for products in other parts of the world. Unless we can achieve a sharp and continuing rise in productivity in this country, our standard of living is bound to fall. In recent years we have been fairly used to a rapid and continuous improvement in our standard of living. Any change in our economic position relative to that of other countries could well require us to accept a much lower rate of improvement over the next decade or so, and thus leave families with a more or less constant standard of living, or even a falling one.

The result of our present economic position is that a number of people are having difficulty in finding employment. School leavers are taking longer to find a job, and when they do it is not always what they would have liked. Executives become redundant in their fifties and are unable to find alternative employment, and skilled workers have found the industry for which they are trained reducing its staff. The effect on the family is not only a reduction in income and therefore in expenditure. Deep psychological harm can result from feelings of insecurity and rejection.

This is a new situation for most families, because government policy since the last war has been to maintain full employment, which has meant in practice that all but those who were changing their jobs or were unemployable were sure of fairly secure employment. The present situation is likely to be intensified in future years. A combination of the need to make the most efficient use of modern production methods and the need to take long-term action to rectify our economic position could well lead to a higher level of unemployment than we have been accustomed to in the post-war period.

This will have its effects on people's way of life. It could mean shorter hours of work, with greater leisure, which might be filled with amusements or taking on another occupation that is not paid in the normal way. Perhaps crafts which have almost died out will be revived, or more time will be given to voluntary service of one sort or another. Young people may be encouraged to stay at school longer, or further education may be increased and diversified so that it will appeal to a larger number of people. This filling of leisure time could prove a difficult problem for the family of the future.

The implementation of the Equal Pay Act, 1970, and the Sex Discrimination Act, 1975, could also have an important effect upon the homes of the future. Equal pay could mean more money coming into the home if the wife goes out to work, and she is encouraged to do so by the Employment Protection Act, 1977. This gives her the right to six weeks' paid maternity leave when she has a baby, and allows her to return to her job, or a similar one, up to twenty-nine weeks after the birth of the child.

If women want to take advantage of these changes, improvements will have to be made in arrangements for caring for the children of working mothers. There will have to be a greater flexibility in working hours to suit women employees with children at school. More convenience foods will need to be manufactured, especially those suitable for babies and young children. Communal services for laundry and heavy household cleaning will have to be provided at a cost that the ordinary worker can afford; and housework will have to be made more labour-saving through the provision of cheaper and more adequate domestic equipment.

There is more to the situation than such practical matters. Complete equality between the sexes can only come about if a profound transformation takes place in social attitudes to family life and responsibilities. Although there has been a great change in relationships within the home in the last decade or so, there is still room for advance. There needs to be full acceptance of the idea that both parents have to do their share of the housework and looking after the children. Politicians have still to be convinced that arrangements to enable mothers to work should be given high priority in government planning and subsidisation; and employers have still to discover that men and women are of equal use in comparable occupations. A social revolution of this sort takes time, but it is possible that these ideas will be quite acceptable to the next generation.

So the home of tomorrow is likely to be one in which comfort and warmth are predominant. Whether it will look anything like the home of today is questionable. If the sensational twelve-storey development by a Canadian architect known as Habitat 67 is anything to go by, it could consist of a pile of single, fully detached family houses, arranged in storeys one on top of another in such a way that each has its own garden, and its own front door leading onto a 'street', with no contact between the ceilings, floors or walls of adjacent houses, and a children's playground in the sky. But this sort of building is for people with money. The ordinary family's home is likely to be prefabricated to save cost, with perhaps a flat roof and a greater use of concrete and plastic as building materials.

The interior of the home will probably have the same specialised rooms as now – a living room, dining room and kitchen, with bedrooms according to need. The way these are furnished could be rather different, largely because the materials will be man-made, and it is impossible to hazard a guess as to design.

Family size may be about the same, though with an increasing number of ageing people for a time. There is likely to be more sharing of household tasks by husband and wife, and fewer things which are confined to one sex or the other. Leisure time occupations will have changed, as they always do. But people will still need the support, the comfort and security of happy relationships within the home to help them face the problems of modern living. It is to be hoped that the home will still be the centre to which the family members are drawn.

Just as the ordinary family faces together the problems which family life produce, this 'togetherness' should extend beyond the family into the neighbourhood and the community. This involves a mutual agreement between friends and neighbours to help one another in times of need, and for family social services to be available to support and extend what cannot be done in this way. There will need to be an acceptance by everyone in the community of everyone else, regardless of class, sex, race and creed, and a desire to help where help is needed. Home, family and community will then be able to achieve a oneness which will help to give the home and family the security and support they need. This is something which our modern society lacks, and which is the only basis upon which a democratic society, that values goodness and truth, can expect to survive.

Further Reading
(*indicates more advanced books)

1 HOME, FAMILY AND SOCIAL CLASS

Fletcher, Ronald	*The Family and Marriage in Britain* (Penguin 1969)
Farmer, Mary	*The Family* (Longman 1970)
Young, M., Willmott, P.	*The Symmetrical Family* (Penguin 1975)

2 THE FAMILY GROUP

*Bowlby, J., Fry, M.	*Child Care and the Growth of Love* (Pelican 1965)
Kahn, J. H.	*Human Growth and Development* (Pergamon 1965)
*Mead, Margaret	*Male and Female* (Penguin 1970)
Newson, J. & E.	*Patterns of Infant Care in an Urban Community* (Penguin 1971)
Pochin, Jean	*Without a Wedding Ring* (Constable 1969)
Young, M., Willmott, P.	*Family and Kinship in East London* (Routledge & Kegan Paul 1969)

3 EARNING AND SPENDING

Adburgham, A.	*Shops and Shopping* (Allen & Unwin 1964)
Harbury, C. D.	*An Introduction to Economic Behaviour* (Fontana 1971)
HMSO	*A Shopper's Guide* (Office of Fair Trading 1976)

4 WORK AND LEISURE

*Anderson, Nels	*Work and Leisure* (Routledge & Kegan Paul 1961)
Oakley, Ann	*Housewife* (Penguin 1976)
*Smith, M.	*Leisure and Society in Britain* (Allen Lane 1974)
Willmott, P.	*Adolescent Boys in East London* (Routledge & Kegan Paul 1966)

5 HOUSING THE FAMILY

Page, D., Muir, T.	*New Housing for the Elderly* (NCSS 1971)

6 THE FAMILY IN A COMMUNITY SETTING

*Batten, T. R.	*Communities and their Development* (Oxford University Press 1968)
Blythe, R.	*Akenfield* (Penguin 1972)
Burgen, T., Edson, P.	*Spring Grove* (Oxford University Press 1970)
Goodenough, S.	*Jam and Jerusalem* (Collins 1977)

148 *Home, Family and Community*

*Klein, J.	*Samples from English Culture* (Routledge & Kegan Paul, 1965)
Mitton, R., Morrison, E.	*A Community Project in Notting Dale* (Allen Lane 1972)
Nicholson, J. H.	*New Communities in Britain* (NCSS 1961)
Rigby, A.	*Communes in Britain* (Routledge & Kegan Paul 1974)

7 SOCIAL SERVICES FOR THE FAMILY

Barr, Alan	*Student Community Action* (NCSS 1972)
*Bruce, Maurice	*The Coming of the Welfare State* (Batsford 1971)
Dartington, Tim	*Task Force* (Mitchell Beazley 1971)
DHSS	*Family Benefits* (1976)
Holman, Robert	*Socially Deprived Families in Britain* (NCSS 1974)
Willmott, Phyllis	*Consumers' Guide to the Social Services* (Penguin 1976)

Periodicals:
Housewife
New Society
Which?

Publications of the National Council for Social Service, the Central Office of Information, and the Institute of Community Studies:
Social Trends, Government Statistical Service (annual)
National Food Survey, Ministry of Agriculture (annual)
General Household Survey, Department of the Environment (occasional)
Family Expenditure Survey, Department of Employment (annual)
Design Papers, Department of the Environment
Equipment for the Disabled, Department of Health and Social Security

Reports:
Barlow Report, *Distribution of Industrial Population* (Cmnd 6153)
Buchanan Report, *Traffic in Towns* (Ministry of Transport 1963)
Finer Report, *One-Parent Families* (Cmnd 3885)
Molony Report, *Consumer Protection*, 1962 (Cmnd 1781)
Parker-Morris Report, *Homes for Today and Tomorrow* (HMSO 1961)

Index

Abbeyfield 127
Adolescence 30, 32
Adult centres 74
Affection 11
Alcoholism 137-8
Anderson, Elizabeth Garrett 64
Arts Council 75

Booker, Ilys 114
Bowlby, John 28
British Standards Institution 60
British Tourist Authority 71, 73, 77
Broadcasting 70, 73
Building societies 82, 88
Burgin and Edson 120

Caravan 77, 96
Cash and carry 56
Cave dwellings 7
Chapman, Dennis 16
Charitable Organisations 7, 18, 130–3; British Legion 130; CHAR 95; Children's Society 137; Dr Barnardo's 18; Family Welfare Association 130; Girls' Friendly Society 124; Gingerbread 134; Red Cross 127, 130; Samaritans 130; Toc H 130; YMCA 124; YWCA 18
Child Benefit Scheme 127
Child Guidance 129
Child Poverty Action Group 140
Children 10, 23, 27–32, 37, 38, 68; Only child 11, 33; Adoption and fostering 33, 136, 137; In care 136
Citizens' Advice Bureaux 59, 61
Clothing 11, 21
Clubs 74
Communes 10–11
Community 112, 145; Community Centre 115; Community Development 113–15; Community Homes 136
Commuters 100, 105
Consumers' Organisations 57–61; Consumers' Advice Centres 61; Consumers' Association 60; Consumers' Council 59
Conurbations 102, 108
Cooking 7, 8, 70, 143
Courting 25, 26
Crafts 44, 75
Credit 57

Culture 15, 21
Customs 11
Cyrenians 139

Delinquency 68, 69
Denman College 133
Deprived areas 117, 120
Design Council 60
Discount houses 56
Divorce and separation 37
Do-it-yourself 57, 70, 72, 74
Domestic equipment 20, 50, 67, 69, 142
Domestic service 18, 20, 64, 67, 68
Drama 74
Drugs 32, 137, 138–9

Earnings 45–6, 145
Eating out 71
EEC 141–2
Elderly 34, 46, 72, 94, 96–8, 124, 127, 140
Electricity 9, 143
Employment 31, 144
Energy conservation 144
Entertaining 70, 73, 118
Environmental Planning 106–8
Expenditure: Government 42; Consumers 46–51

Family 9, 10–14; Contemporary 18–21, 22; Deprived 133–9; Establishment of 25–7; Immigrant 21–2, 120–1; Life 20, 99, 144; Relationships 23–5; Single-parent 11, 36–9, 95, 124–5, 134; Social provision for 127–30; Span 19; Type 12–13; 34
Family Income Supplement 134
Family Service Units 135
Farming 11, 99, 105
Feminism 20
Flats 67, 92, 93–4, 97
Food 28; Convenience 7–8, 49, 69, 71; School meals 128; Taboos 21
Friends 9, 30, 70

Gardening 20, 70
Government Departments: Environment 77, 143; Food, Ministry of 132; Health and Social Security 123; Treasury 77
Groups: Primary 23–4; Pressure 24, 39, 139

Index

Handicapped 34–6, 96, 124, 126, 128
Happiness 33
Health 20, 27, 29
Health visitor 127–8
Heating 9, 47, 76
Hire purchase 56
Holidays 63, 71, 77
Home 7–10, 19, 69, 76, 141
Home help 124
Hospital 96, 126
Hotel 72
Household 13, 46, 47, 69, 83
Houses: Council 19, 82, 87–8, 89–90; owner-occupied 84, 89; prefabricated 45, 82; privately rented 84, 85, 90
Housewife 49, 142
Housework 19, 118
Housing Chapter 5, 38, 47, 48, 144; Design 91–4, 145–6; Estates 19, 67, 107, 115; Loans 84, 88, 90–1; Management 88; Policy 79–84; Repair 90–1; Standards 89–91, 96
Housing Associations 95
Howard, Ebenezer 106
Husband 13, 19, 26

Immigrants 15, 21–2, 120–1
Income: Disposable 42; Family 11, 18, 47–8, 49, 50, 134
Income Tax 43
Industrial revolution 16, 17, 62, 64, 101, 122
Infant 28, 34
Inflation 46, 70, 142
Institute of Community Studies 13
Irish 21

Jews 21
Justice of the Peace 133

Kerr, Madeline 117
Kibbutz 10
Kinship 12
Klein, Viola 68
Knitting 74

Landlords 80, 88, 120
Launderettes 57
Leisure activities 67–72; Industries 72–5; Planning of 75–8
Local authority 47, 61, 80, 88, 95, 98, 139
Local councillor 133
Loneliness 67, 94, 112, 118
Longhouse 12

Market research 57
Marriage 13, 19, 26, 33, 38, 123
Maternity and child welfare 127–8
Mead, Margaret 24
Mennonites 14
Mental health 124, 126, 134
Mitton and Morrison 114
Motels 57
Mother 10, 24, 28, 35, 36, 67
Mothers' Union 106, 133
Museums 78
Music 74

National Council of Social Service 115, 131
National Council of Women 132
National economy 40–4
National Food Survey 48
National Health Service 125, 139
National Marriage Guidance Council 129
National Trust 77
Needlework 74
Neighbourhood 115–17, 118, 120
Neighbours 117, 118, 146
'New' towns 19, 107–8, 114, 118
Newson, John and Elizabeth 28
Nursing 64, 65

Occupation 44, 92
Old-age pensioner 47, 49
OPEC 143
Open University 72

Pakistan 21, 25
Paneth, Marie 117
Parent 20, 25, 27, 29, 33, 120, 145
Parks 72
Parliamentary Acts: Caravan sites 96; Children and young persons 136, 137; Chronically Sick and Disabled Persons 96, 126; Clean Air 110; Education 128; Equal Pay 145; Fair Trading 59; Food and Drugs 58, 59; House Purchase 91; Housing Finance 95; Litter 110; Local Authority Social Services 124; Matrimonial Causes 64; Mental Health 126; Misrepresentation 58; National Assistance 95, 137–8; National Health Service 125; Rent 95; Town and Country Planning 106, 110; Trade Descriptions 58; Unsolicited Goods 58
Personality 32
Pets 76
Plastics 51, 70

Pollution 110, 142
Population 141
Property 43

Rathbone, Eleanor 127
Reading 69, 74
Recycling 143
Refuse disposal 110
Relationships 9, 23–5, 29, 67
Relatives 13, 32, 34
Rents 47, 87
Reports of Committees and Commissions: Barlow 117; Beveridge 122, 129; Buchanan 110; Census of Distribution 51; Environmental Pollution 110; Family Expenditure Survey 46: Gaitskell 52; Housing of the Working Classes 80; Ince 129; Lane 137; Molony 59; National Food Survey 48; Newson 75; Parker-Morris 89; Planning for Leisure 62; Piercy 96; Seebohm 124
Retail marketing 51–7
Roads 111
Roles 31, 33
Rural areas 15, 25, 50, 98, 103–6, 143; communities 103–6

School 21, 23, 35, 61, 75, 93, 120, 128, 129, 134
Scouts 24
Shift-work 63
Shopping 52, 93
Shops: Co-op 52; Departmental stores 53; High Street 51, 56; Mobile 56; Multiple 52, 54; Self-service 54; Shopping-centre 56; Supermarket 54–5
Single-women 39
Smoking 138
Society 14, 15, 21, 30, 31, 39, 62, 113
Social change 13, 31, 83
Social Class 15–17, 69, 83, 117, 145; Upper 15; Middle 17, 45, 63, 118; Working 17, 18, 19, 119
Social responsibility 139–40
Social services Chapter 7, 14
Soviet Union 66
Standard of living 11, 18, 44, 88

State control 45
Suburbs 15, 100, 116, 135

Taxation 43–4
Technology 20, 45
Teenagers 43, 48, 51, 93
Television 69–70, 73
Temporary accommodation 95
Tenants 80, 85, 93, 95
Tied cottage 79
Toilet training 28
Tourism 73
Toys 40
Theatre 75
Trade Unions 46, 62
Traffic 110–11
Transport: Motor 105; Public 111

Urban growth 108–12
Urban society 11, 101

Vending machines 57
Voluntary Service Overseas 131
Voluntary work 171, 130–1
Volunteers 130–3

Wage differentials 45
Walking 72
War 44, 82, 89, 141
Waste 143
Weight-watching 131
West Indians 15, 21
Welfare State 122–7, 139
Which? 60
Widows 131
Wife 13, 26, 65, 66–9
Women: Leisure 63–4; Occupation 45; Politics 65
Women's Institute 106, 133
Work 31, 44–6, 62–9
WRVS 127, 132

Young and Willmott 20, 69, 117
Young Farmers' Clubs 105
Youth Employment 129
Youth Service 74